KOOTENAY
NATIONAL PARK

Bob Hahn

Front cover: Subalpine larches at Wolverine Pass.
Tumbling Glacier in the background. Photo Bob Hahn.
Back cover: Looking into the Kootenay River valley. Photo Bob Hahn.
Title page and contents page photo Bob Hahn.

Photographs provided by Kootenay National Park
unless otherwise credited.

We acknowledge the financial support of the Government of
Canada through the Book Publishing Industry Development
Program (BPIDP) for our publishing activities.

Printed and bound in Canada by
Houghton Boston, Saskatoon

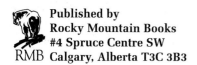

Published by
Rocky Mountain Books
#4 Spruce Centre SW
RMB **Calgary, Alberta T3C 3B3**

ISBN 0-921102-74-7

Canadian Cataloguing in Publication Data

Hahn, Bob, 1937-
  Kootenay National Park

  Includes index.
  ISBN 0-921102-74-7

  1. Kootenay National Park (B.C.)--Guidebooks. I. Title.
FC3814.K68H34 2000   917.11'65   C00-910305-8
F1089.K68H34 2000

Contents

Acknowledgments

I'm indebted to many of my park colleagues and friends for their support and editorial counsel, but especially Larry Halverson, who had enough confidence in my abilities to get this project rolling, John Pitcher, who did his best to keep me on the straight and narrow, Ross MacDonald, a man of action and Marla Oliver, whose perseverance and hard work finally made this book become a reality. Thanks to Ben Gadd for the fine editing and for writing the foreword. I also appreciate the patience and efforts of publisher Tony Daffern and his staff. A special thanks to Gillean Daffern for her photo contributions. My gratitude is extended to the Friends of Kootenay National Park for their belief in me. They made it all possible. Lastly, I sincerely appreciate the assistance and unlimited (usually) support of my partner in many an outdoor adventure, my wife, Catherine Irene.

Dedication

Dedicated to the memory of my father whose dreams of living close to nature became my reality.

Foreword

I met Bob Hahn quite a few years ago. Two things struck me immediately about him: he was deaf as a post and he was a very funny guy.

Quips, that's what Bob was good at. He still is. And it shows in his writing: "Radium has a motel for every day of the month." "Toad attacks are virtually unknown in Kootenay National Park."

In my favourite, Bob instructs on the differences between species of conifers in the park: "Squeeze a bunch [of needles] with your hand. You can even do it with your eyes closed. If you say "Ouch!" it's a Sharp Spruce; if not, you've just met a Friendly Fir. If it growls, you don't have a tree at all. Good luck."

Bob can also chuckle at what park visitors have told him. He passes some of his favourites on to us: "Can you tell me the location of any undiscovered lakes in the park?" "How high does a sheep have to get before it becomes a goat?"

There's a lot more than humour in this book, of course. Bob has spent 12 summers as a park interpreter in Kootenay National Park. He puts all that experience into the tome before you, making it by far the best naturalist's and recreationist's guide to the region.

In these pages you'll find detail on the park's botany and life zones. There's a full section on wildlife, from moose to marmots and bighorns to bunnies. Bob supplements the straight information with fascinating critter lore, including bear stories and cougar stories to relate around the campfire. Read about weasels playing tag at Olive Lake (page 48), or the honest-to-goodness boa constrictor of the Rockies (page 131).

And there are some fine park-people stories as well. On page 94 you can find out how warden Brian Sheehan rescued a St. Bernard dog that fell into Marble Canyon. Read also "The warden and the wolves," page 106.

There is plenty of info. on the things Kootenay is best known for—Radium Hot Springs, the Paint Pots, Marble Canyon—with maps to get you there and road logs to keep you entertained along the way. Bob has hiked the whole park, and his trail descriptions are first-rate.

This book reaches beyond the national park. It deals with the surrounding Columbia Valley region, from Canal Flats to Golden. Included are items on the world-class wetlands of the Columbia National Wildlife area, the neighbouring Purcell Mountains, etc.

Bob is a fine photographer. Many of the lovely illustrations in *Kootenay National Park* are his own.

The book ends with a quote from Larry Halverson, perhaps the area's best-known naturalist. It comes from the heart: "If folks have good experiences in the wild, those memories might come to mind when landscapes are threatened—making those same people defenders of the places they cherish."

Indeed. Bob Hahn's work will help. Good on ya, Bob. I said, *"GOOD ON YA, BOB!"*

Ben Gadd

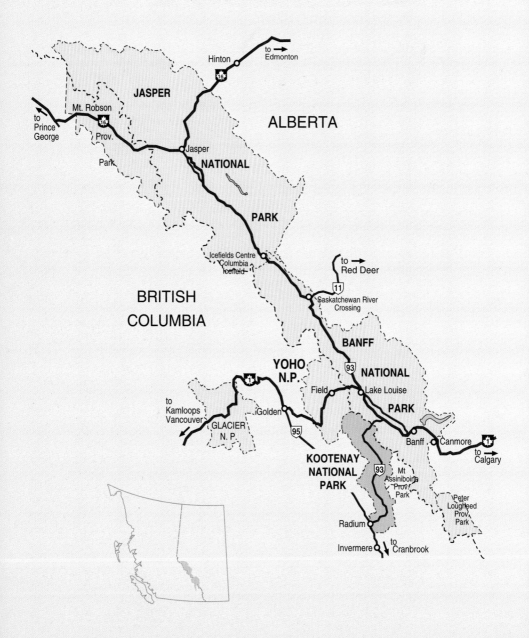

Welcome to Kootenay National Park

Photo Bob Hahn.

Kootenay National Park—A Very Special Place

Floe Lake. Photo Gillean Daffern.

On the Banff side, water flows into the Bow River, then into the Saskatchewan River system and on to Hudson Bay. West of the Divide, in Kootenay National Park, water drains first into the Vermilion River, then enters the Kootenay River and finally the Columbia, which empties into the Pacific Ocean at Astoria, Oregon.

The park is approximately 85 km from north to south, with an average width of 15 km (the maximum is 25 km). Total area is 1406 km². Shape and size are primarily determined by the 94 km of Highway 93, the Kootenay Parkway, which traverses the park. For most of its length, the highway parallels either the Kootenay or Vermilion rivers.

Like so many others, I first came to Kootenay because it was on the way to Banff. We spent one night in the village of Radium Hot Springs and then hurried on to the more well-known attractions of Banff. We overlooked most of the attributes that make Kootenay such a special place. Many years passed before I realized just how much we had missed.

Where else can you find a park that contains both cactus and glaciers? It certainly won't be in Canada. Can you envision a more spectacular entrance to any park than Sinclair Canyon? There are grizzly bears, two species of lions, even elephants. However, I must confess that the most common "lions" are tiny insects (ant lions), and that the elephants—pink, yet—only move when a breeze ruffles their alpine flowerbeds.

Kootenay has no Grand Canyon, but Marble Canyon is a worthy substitute. In the same way, those who yearn for warm sandy beaches

Kootenay National Park is the southernmost of four contiguous Rocky Mountain parks. The others are Banff, Jasper and Yoho. Together with three adjoining British Columbia provincial parks—Mount Assiniboine, Mount Robson and Hamber—these parks have been designated a World Heritage Site by the United Nations. This spectacular area, with its abundance of wildlife, is one of the larger protected areas on the globe.

Kootenay is bordered on the north by Yoho, and on the east by Banff and Mount Assiniboine. The Continental Divide forms the division between Kootenay and Banff.

might be disappointed, but close your eyes while soaking in the 40°C water of the Radium Hot Springs Pools and you can almost hear palm fronds whispering overhead. As for all those tropical flowers, there's no need to head south to find orchids—22 different species grow in the park! And you can search for them without having to worry about poisonous snakes. Keep your eyes peeled for Kootenay's boa constrictors, though. Rubber boas are infrequently found in the vicinity of the hot pools.

If you really want to experience wilderness serenity, you're more likely to find it in Kootenay than in some of the better-known parks. The number of backcountry campers is strictly limited and over 250 km of trails lead to places like 350 m-high Helmet Falls and the internationally famous Rockwall. In the summer, hikers marvel at the floral beauty of alpine meadows, while autumn trekkers are dazzled by the golden display of subalpine larches.

Yes, Kootenay National Park has numerous features that make it a unique treasure, but this holds true for all of Canada's national parks. Ultimately, Parks Canada intends to protect representative examples of each of the countries' 39 natural terrestrial landscapes. Almost two-thirds of that goal has been realized.

Attitudes have changed drastically since the discovery of hot springs on the east slope of the Rockies led to the establishment of Banff, Canada's first national park, in 1885. The formation of the park had nothing to do with conservation and preservation. Representatives of the federal government and officers of the Canadian Pacific Railway saw only dollar signs when they looked at the springs. Plans were to make the area a "pleasuring ground for the rich."

That was only one of many mistakes made in the development of Canada's outstanding system of national parks, but errors were to be expected in the beginning. It was a different time and the whole idea of national parks was a new concept. It wasn't until 1930, with the passage of the National Parks Act, that Canadian parks were even protected from logging, mining and other commercial ventures. And it took a further 58 years before stiffer amendments to the act gave priority to the "maintenance of ecological integrity through protection of natural resources." In other words: "Is it good for the ecosystem?"

Obviously, ecosystems—meaning the interaction of communities of plants and animals with their environments—weren't considered when park boundaries were established. Now we realize that Kootenay is only a small part of the Central Rockies Ecosystem, an area the size of Switzerland. In order to ensure that all native species are thriving in as natural a state as possible—something called ecological integrity—the park cannot exist as a separate entity. Kootenay's wilderness is always at risk from access and developments on adjacent provincial lands.

While some backcountry areas are threatened, there is no comparison to the pressure in the valleys. These are the transportation corridors and the site of most development. With park visitors coming in ever-increasing numbers, maintaining ecological integrity in the face of internal development becomes more difficult. Highway improvements and the provision of tourist facilities are examples. Compounding the problem is the high cost of operating our parks. The number one priority of national parks is protection, and that doesn't come cheaply.

We once thought life would go on as it always had within park boundaries—even with a few more humans tromping around. But lines drawn on a map do not deter wind, water nor wolves. The key to ecological integrity within Kootenay and the other parks depends on how well we look after the entire ecosystem. It's a daunting job.

On your trip through the park, take time to wander a few trails, smell the flowers, enjoy our quiet campgrounds and maybe even take in an evening program. Hopefully, you'll begin to develop feelings similiar to mine—that Kootenay National Park is a valuable jewel in the crown of the Rocky Mountains. But always bear in mind that unlike a diamond, Kootenay cannot survive alone.

Who Came First and Why?

It was once believed the Kootenay or Ktunaxa (tun-ah-hah) people (the first term is actually an Anglicized version of the latter, which means people from beyond the hills) weren't permanent residents of the area until the 1700s. However, most archeologists, as well as the Ktunaxa themselves, are now convinced the tribe has been here for 10,000 years or more. It only seems logical to assume an area as rich in wildlife as the Kootenay and Vermilion River valleys has been populated much longer than 300 years.

It is known that the Ktunaxa regularly crossed the Rockies via White Man Pass (south of the park boundary), Simpson Pass and Vermilion Pass to hunt buffalo on the plains. Aboriginal peoples also used the Kootenay River route as a north-south travel corridor, especially when trading posts on the North Saskatchewan River were established.

There is little doubt the Ktunaxa bathed in Radium Hot Springs—perhaps to ease the pain of arthritis or to help cleanse and heal injuries received in battle. A number of other tribes, such as the Peigans, Bloods and Stoneys, may have also come to soak in the hot water. The presence of pictographs near the hot springs (unfortunately destroyed by construction) was a possible indication that aboriginal peoples found the area sacred. Another sacred area was the Paint Pots, which was also of economic benefit to First Nations people (see page 83).

Undoubtedly, the first non-native people in the area were trappers and fur traders, but the initial recorded visit was by Sir George Simpson in 1841. Simpson was governor of the Hudson's Bay Company, and he was trying to go around the world in record time. He came into the Vermilion River drainage via the pass later named after him (by James Hector in 1858), travelled down the Kootenay and crossed to the Columbia through what is now called Sinclair Pass.

Simpson was a man in a hurry. Like too many modern travellers who want to see all the Rocky Mountain parks in a few days, he didn't spend much time here. In an era when other expeditions might take months to cross the country (the 1857 Palliser Expedition took an entire year to travel from Lake Superior to the Rockies), Simpson crossed the Rockies in only five days. In fact, he drove his men so hard they called him "the little emperor"—but probably not to his face. Yet, this short visit is immortalized not only by the place names

The Ktunaxa were the first permanent residents of the area.

12

but by a monument (see page 71) near the junction of the Simpson and Vermilion rivers.

Following in Simpson's footprints was James Sinclair. Sinclair, although not a member of the Hudson's Bay Company (he didn't join them until 1883), had agreed to guide 23 families from Fort Garry (now Winnipeg) to Walla Walla, Washington. The purpose was to establish a foothold for the company in the fur-rich areas south of the 49th parallel. He actually left Fort Garry before Simpson, but "the little emperor" overtook the cavalcade en route. Simpson had directed Sinclair to undertake the perilous journey, and arranged for the party to travel through Athabasca Pass in what is now Jasper National Park.

After Simpson rushed off to continue his round-the-world journey, James Sinclair chose to ignore the governor's directions. Sinclair had disagreed with the company before, especially in their treatment of the Métis of the Red River area. Thus, he elected to journey south and found his own route through the Rockies (White Man Pass). Upon reaching the Kootenay River valley, he followed Simpson's footsteps over the western range and down past the hot springs. If Sinclair had travelled according to plan, a stream and pass wouldn't bear his name, let alone a canyon.

Another early visitor to the Columbia Valley was Father Pierre de Smet. In 1845, Father de Smet followed Sinclair's route in reverse by going up Sinclair Creek, crossing the Kootenay River and following the Cross River up to White Man Pass. There he supposedly erected a small cross, which led to the naming of the river. Father de Smet also erected another cross, which can be seen in the church on the Shuswap

Pictographs near the hot springs were destroyed during construction of the pools.

Indian Reserve south of the village of Radium Hot Springs.

The only other noteworthy exploration of the area came with the Palliser Expedition of 1857-1860. The British government sent Captain John Palliser to determine how feasible the area was for future development. One member of his party, geologist James Hector, led a branch of the expedition on several excursions into this part of the Rockies, naming many of the features. Hector is credited with being the first non-native to cross Vermilion Pass (1858). In fact, he noted the pass was the most feasible route of any he had seen for "wheeled conveyances." On that trip he ended up in what is now Yoho National Park, where he was kicked in the chest by a horse and taken for dead—but miraculously recovered. That's how Yoho came to have both the Kicking Horse River and Kicking Horse Pass.

Historical notes about the Kootenay area for the next twenty-some years are absent, until John McKay staked a homestead along the Columbia River in the 1880s. His claim happened to include Radium Hot Springs.

Snow has never deterred bathers at the hot springs. Note the early "bathhouse."

Expansion of the pool became necessary as the number of park visitors increased.

History of the Radium Hot Pools

Most sources list Roland Stuart, an English squire, as the first legally registered owner of the hot springs. Stuart paid the munificent sum of $1 an acre to receive a Crown grant for the 160 acres surrounding the pool. He was the first to see the economic potential of the springs, but initially he expected to reap his rewards from sales of the bottled water, not from bathers.

In 1911 a British medical journal suggested there might be radium in the water. (By coincidence, that was also the first year it became possible to drive to the springs—see the next section.) Research by McGill University in

1913 showed this to be true. Stuart realized his slightly radioactive spring water might have more curative power than the famous springs at Bath, England. He envisioned even more financial possibilities—if he could come up with enough money for development. That dilemma was solved, at least temporarily, by multimillionaire St. John Harmsworth. Harmsworth was paralyzed from the neck down when he first came to Radium Hot Springs, and spent several hours each day suspended in the hot water. After four months of treatment, he could move his feet. That meant a $20,000 contribution to Stuart, who constructed a concrete pool and a log bathhouse before heading for England at the start of the First World War.

Stuart still hadn't returned in 1920 when negotiations between the federal and provincial governments were concluded and the formation of Kootenay Dominion Park was announced. Stuart's agent, Earle Scovil, couldn't get any communication from his boss, and encouraged the government to expropriate the springs. The feds did as Scovil suggested in 1922, a year before the Banff-Windermere Road was completed. Stuart eventually received about $40,000 for his $160 investment, but even at that time others placed the value of the springs at half a million dollars.

In the years to follow, the pool was modified slightly and a more elaborate bathhouse was built. The bathhouse burned down during the winter of 1948 and was replaced by the present stone building. The new facilities, including a second (cool) pool, that was two-thirds Olympic size, were officially opened in 1951. And the hot springs permanently disappeared

This bathhouse burned down in 1948 and was replaced by the present stone building.

from the public's eyes under the concrete of the hot pool.

Major renovations during the winter of 1967/68 meant removal of the old pool and the installation of a collecting system for all the hot water sources. The changes created a slight decrease in water temperature to the present 40°C.

Another round of renovations, initiated in 1997, primarily altered the building, but a hot/cold plunge pool was also added.

More information on the hot pools is available in the book *Nipika*, sold at information centres and at the pools.

Chemical Composition of the Pools

Water from the springs is slightly radioactive, similar to the famous mineral springs in Bath, England. There is no sulphur to cause the unpleasant smell associated with many hot springs.

Chemical	Parts per million
Sulphate	302.00
Calcium	135.00
Bicarbonate	100.80
Silica	31.80
Magnesium	31.60
Sodium	18.40
Alumina & iron oxide	3.60
Nitrate	0.60
Fluoride	0.37
Chloride	0.17

As if the Water Wasn't Hot Enough

In May of 1967 a tank truck went out of control coming down the highway, crashed into Sinclair Creek above the pools and exploded, killing the driver. Six thousand gallons of burning fuel raced downstream. At that time the creek ran between the hot pool and the bathhouse. Although some bathers suffered minor burns, no one was seriously injured.

Flames roared so high that trees on the slope above the hot pool were set on fire. You can still determine the size of the fire by the extent of deciduous trees that have since replaced burned conifers.

Whose Idea was this Kootenay Park, Anyhow?

Travel in the Columbia Valley prior to 1900 was primarily north-south. But settlers led by Robert Bruce, an Invermere business man, began clamoring for a more direct route to markets in Banff and Calgary. This led to a meeting with the premier of British Columbia and a proposal to build a road via the Vermilion and Kootenay River valleys, crossing Vermilion Pass as Hector had recommended in 1858.

Construction from the Columbia Valley began in 1911, and for the first time there was a road to the hot springs. No attempt was made to en-

The original road through lower Sinclair Canyon ran side by side with Sinclair Creek.

Construction of the highway began in 1911.

ter the canyon, instead, the new road followed an old packtrail around the defile. In the next few years the road was pushed almost over Sinclair Pass, but lack of funding and a raging conflict on the other side of the world brought work to a stop.

By 1919 the "war to end wars" was over, but the road was far from complete. The province didn't have enough funds to finish the work, so a deal was made with the federal government. The Banff-Windermere Road Agreement stipulated that the feds would build the highway in exchange for 5 mi. (8 km) of land on either side of the road for a national park. The park became a reality in 1920, three years before the road to Castle Junction in Banff National Park was completed.

Looking back, the choice of Vermilion Pass and the two river valleys for the highway seems logical. But why Sinclair Pass? There are other passes both to the north and south that would seem to be more feasible routes. However, none had hot springs along the way—hot springs owned by a silver-tongued Roland Stuart with friends in high places.

The first road over the Canadian Rockies became a reality, and the nation gained a new national park.

Mountains and Carpets—Laying the Foundation

Picture a big rug. Put one side against the wall and push on the opposite edge. The carpet rises in folds, but it never breaks. Now, imagine the earth's crust as the carpet—but let's add more layers—layers of rock. These layers have formed in the shallow water at the edge of the Pacific Ocean. They are composed of material eroded from old mountain ranges, plus the calcareous skeletons of countless aquatic invertebrates. At least that's the simplified version of where I always thought those layers of sedimentary rock came from—the same version that unsuspecting visitors had been getting from me for years—just as if I actually knew something about geology.

But after seven years, something started to bother me (besides my conscience). I always ended any Stanley Glacier hike (see page 99) by showing fossil evidence of aquatic invertebrates to my group as proof of a rehearsed spiel recited earlier in the day. But I could never locate fossils on any of the other guided hikes. Certainly fossils can be found in many other areas of the park, but why aren't they more numerous? They're supposed to be the major component of limestone rock that forms most of the Canadian Rockies, aren't they? Why can you inspect slab after slab of rock on some mountains and find nary a fossil?

Lo and behold, a little digging in Ben Gadd's Handbook of the Canadian Rockies turned up some interesting facts about the formation of limestone. Even geologists were puzzled until the 1950s. Then they found that certain types of salt-water algae produce minute particles of calcium carbonate ($CaCO_3$—calcite) that settle to the bottom when the algae die.

Of course, algae are too soft to form a fossil, so animals have gotten all the credit. Yet, skeletal remains form only a very small portion of the limestone. It just goes to show that if you don't leave a few obvious signs, people tend to ignore you.

So, let's see—we've got tonnes of material collecting on the bottom of a shallow sea. After a few million years it's pretty thick, and the pressure at the bottom is so great things begin to heat up and all those sediments are squeezed together tighter than rush-hour commuters on a subway. Eventually they end up as sedimentary limy rock.

Restless Rocks

Now, let's dig a little deeper. Everybody knows the centre of the earth is quite a bit warmer than your Saturday night bath (that also has a lot to do with pressure from the weight above). If you aren't sure about that, stick your toe in the hot pool. The water in the pool seeped down just far enough to become steam (maybe 2.5 km), and then reversed course (see page 14). Imagine the heat at 100 km, 1000 km or all the way to the centre, 6336 km. At a great enough depth even the rocks begin to run. With all that heat, and liquid rock, the centre of the earth is far from static. It's more like a vat of boiling pudding. Yet, even though the hot pudding may be convulsing and churning, there is usually a pattern in the movements. Mix up a batch of pudding and throw in a few stale cookies. See if their journeys don't follow a pattern. (The good thing about this experiment is you can usually find some hungry friends to clean up.)

Rise of the Rockies

In a manner similiar to the movement of cookies in our hot pudding, currents in the earth's core move the harder, cooler rock layers above. These layers are divided into sections known as tectonic plates. The plates underlie the continents and even the oceans. About 200 million years ago, the plate underneath what is now North America, which had been drifting slowly eastward, changed directions. As it backed up, it ran over the plate underneath the Pacific Ocean, and in the process began scraping islands and reefs (the result of earlier volcanic activity) off the oceanic plate. The farther the continent went, the more land piled up on its western edge. It was like pushing a snow shovel down the walk, and watching the snow collect on the shovel. If the snow is wet enough, it becomes compressed.

Now we're back to the carpet! The accumulation of land to the west meant less room to the east, and those rock layers, those old compressed masses of skeletons, algae, sand, gravel, etc., started to fold like our rug. And the only way to go was up. In the formation of the Rockies, the layers may have risen as high as the Himalayas, but it wasn't any quick cataclysmic event like an earthquake or volcanic erup-tion. The whole process took tens of millions of years—years of wind and rain, freezing, thawing—all the same erosional forces that are constantly at work today. Thus, even as the mountains were bulldozed higher, that soft limestone was being continuously worn down.

Strangely, all that pushing and shoving between a rock and a hard place is harder on rocks than it is on carpets. The rock layers didn't just fold. Oh, no! There was cracking, breaking (faulting) and even shattering. Some layers not only broke, but were forced right over the tops of others. These *thrust faults* are very obvious in mountains near the Banff townsite. There is also an excellent example in the lower end of Sinclair Canyon.

It wasn't an orderly process— few natural processes are. There were layers folded up into *anti-clines*, and layers folded down into *synclines*, layers forced into contortions that seem impossible in such an apparently stiff medium as rock. But rock under the enormous pressure of mountain building exerted over a long period of time will do amazing things. It all added up to our beautifully complex, but ever changing, Rocky Mountains.

Then came the glaciers.

Nature's Frigid Sculptors

So you think last winter was cold? Your grandpa says it didn't even come close to some of the ones when he was a kid—like the winter when it got so cold that all the words froze. What a racket when conversations thawed in the spring! Actually, it wasn't all that much before grandpa's time when the last Ice Age in the Canadian Rockies was happening. The Cavell glaciation, which is the Rockies equivalent of Europe's Little Ice Age, reached its maximum in the mid-1800s, and the glaciers didn't retreat much until the 1920s. Of course, North America's Little Ice Age (as the Cavell is also called) wasn't like the major ice ages of many, many grandpas ago when ice sheets covered much of North America.

All the ice didn't melt, even when temperatures warmed up. There are still plenty of glaciers hanging on in the Rockies and other parts of the world. However, for the most part, there is no comparison to the volume of ice that was once contained in the continental ice sheets. Even so, about 75 per cent of the world's supply of fresh water remains locked up as ice. That fact may prove to be vitally important to the future of life on earth.

The importance of glaciers in the Canadian Rockies, besides being the major source of water for rivers and lakes, is their sculpting ability. As I mentioned previously, erosion was wearing down the mountains even as they were still being pushed higher. However, the slow abrasion of wind and rain has a tendency to round off rough edges in the same manner as sandpaper when applied to a chunk of wood. Thus the older mountains of the world are usually low and gentle.

Tumbling Glacier is still sculpting the Rockwall.

Obviously, our relatively young Rockies, with their abundance of sharp peaks, narrow ridges and sheer cliffs, have been altered by other forces. That's where the glaciers come in.

What is a glacier? Where does it come from? Glaciers are found in areas where there is too much snowfall in the winter to melt over the summer. Wherever mountain ranges force moisture-laden air currents to rise and cool, as in the Canadian Rockies, precipitation in the form of sleet, hail or snow can whiten the peaks any time of the year. On high alpine slopes, especially those that face northeast, the same snow can remain for years and eventually become solid ice. Inevitably, when the ice depth exceeds 30 m, volume and pressure cannot be denied and the collective body of ice may begin to move. If it does, a glacier is born.

While glaciers are still at work in the Rockies, the major sculpting began over two million years ago. But numerous other ice ages have

Stanley Glacier is found in a hanging valley. Photo Bob Hahn.

most impressive of glacier-carved peaks: Matterhorn-like peaks such as Mount Assiniboine, the best-known example in the area (see page 74). Another good example is Mount Verendrye, which is closer to the highway (see page 77). Horn peaks are created when a minimum of three glaciers work on different sides of a mountain, carving toward each other until a horn-shaped spur of rock remains. If a pair of glaciers grind away on opposite sides of a ridge, the effect is the same as sharpening a knife. Sometimes there is barely enough room left at the top to walk single file.

Glaciers are responsible for many of our mountain attractions, from the cliffs that climbers risk their necks on to most of our lovely mountain lakes. Generally, the lakes form behind rock debris (moraines) left by a retreating glacier. Other lakes are dammed up behind rockslides.

When we speak of a glacier retreating, it doesn't mean that it has shifted into reverse. Glaciers always move forward at a fairly constant pace, but at a certain elevation the annual rate of snow accumulation is equal to the annual rate of melting. Then the glacier seems to be standing still. However, in an exceptionally warm, dry year the ice melts faster than the glacier advances—and the icy river appears to be retreating. Just the opposite can happen in a cool, wet year.

At the present time, most glaciers in the Rocky Mountains are shrinking in size, primarily owing to warmer average temperatures. If this trend continues—and many scientists predict that it will unless we reduce the amount of carbon dioxide entering the atmosphere—future park visitors will only see the results of glaciers. The ice will be gone!

come and gone since. During some of these frigid times, the only evidence of land underneath the ice was the tips of the highest peaks sticking out like islands in the sea. These are known as *nunataks*. Obviously, glaciers don't move very fast (the average in the Rockies is about 15 m/year), but when you're talking about 100,000 years, the length of the Great Glaciation (Illinoian), a whole lot of grinding can go on.

The largest glaciers carved out broad U-shaped valleys like those that contain the Vermilion and Kootenay rivers. Smaller glaciers filled the side valleys between the peaks. However, not having the volume of the major glaciers, the little glaciers couldn't carve as deeply and their valleys were left "hanging." Stanley Glacier (see page 99) formed one of these hanging valleys. Some of our larger and more beautiful waterfalls drop from the edges of hanging valleys. Helmet Falls, 350 m high, is unquestionably the most spectacular example in Kootenay.

Spectacular is also the only word to describe what is probably the

Lots of Big Rocks Here

Like the rest of the Canadian Rockies, most of Kootenay National Park is underlain by sedimentary rock, mostly limestone and quartzite. There are three principle mountain divisions, but a look at the map shows even more ranges. The higher peaks are found along the northeast boundary. They include Deltaform Mountain (at 3424 m, Kootenay's highest), and Mounts Allen (3310 m), Tuzo (3245 m) and Fay (3234 m). These four peaks, and a half dozen more, lie along the border of Banff National Park and form the famous backdrop to Moraine Lake: the Valley of the Ten Peaks. Kootenay's largest glacier lies on the south side of these peaks, but doesn't even have a name. The fact that such a natural wonder still remains nameless at the beginning of the 21st century is a good indication of the magnitude and richness of the region.

The Vermilion and Mitchell ranges form the spine of Kootenay. One of the most prominent features of the Vermilion Range is the Rockwall, a vertical barrier of limestone that guards the northwestern boundary of the park. Hiking the Rockwall is one of the must-dos in Kootenay, and four backcountry campsites (see page 79) are located along a 30 km stretch of the wall. Here are found the highest peaks in this area: Mount Foster (3204 m), Helmet Mountain (3139 m) and Mount Verendrye (3086 m). The park's highest and most spectacular waterfall, Helmet Falls (350 m), is an added attraction.

The Mitchell Range forms most of the southeastern boundary of the park. Magnificent peaks like Mount Harkin (2983 m) form a spectacular backdrop to the Kootenay River valley.

The ranges that are found on the southwestern boundary, Brisco and Stanford, are the most complex geologically. Although the highest peaks, Kindersley and Sinclair, don't reach 2700 m, the drive from the west park entrance to Sinclair Pass is one of the steepest in the Canadian Rockies. In addition, this narrow, twisting valley shows little sign of the glaciation that made most of the other valleys in the park wide and straight.

The southwestern corner of Kootenay includes dry benches bordering the Rocky Mountain Trench. The trench is a major valley that extends from the U.S. border to the Yukon. It is such a prominent geological landmark that astronauts in outer space asked about it on an early mission. Even the mighty Columbia is confined by the trench, following it for over 160 km north before the river pierces the barrier and turns south (see page 141). In the segment bordering Kootenay, this valley marks a major break in the earth's crust. The valley has dropped several kilometres, but rivers are working to fill up the gap. The streams are constantly depositing large amounts of sand and gravel eroded from the mountain ranges bordering the trench.

The Rockwall is a vertical barrier of limestone that stretches more than 50 km along the northwest corner of the park. Photo Bob Hahn.

A Little Background Music

Kootenay National Park is primarily made up of three main ecoregions: montane, subalpine and alpine. The southern tip of the park also contains a brief portion of a unique dry section of the montane associated with the Rocky Mountain Trench. Although there is no clear boundary between regions—rarely are natural boundries well defined—each has its own characteristics in terms of rainfall, temperature, flora, fauna and other factors.

Driving through the park from southwest to northeast, you briefly pass through the **dry montane** area before climbing into the more typical **montane**. Beyond Kootenay Crossing, about halfway through the park, you enter the **subalpine**. Visitors to the highest ecoregion, the **alpine**, must travel on their own two feet. There are no roads.

The Dry Montane

This is the only place in Canada where you will find any environment comparable to that of the Rocky Mountain Trench protected in a national park. The most unusual resident of this arid habitat is the prickly pear cactus, which grows just inside the southwest boundary of the park. Growing alongside the cactus are other typical dry country plants like sagebrush and rabbitbrush. However, it's the bunchgrass, flourishing on the west-facing slopes, that has always been vital to wintering Rocky Mountain bighorn sheep. Unfortunately, forest succession—trees invading the open slopes—has caused a decline in this traditional winter range.

The Montane

In this area of the Rocky Mountains, the montane zone ranges from an elevation of about 1000 m to anywhere from 1500 m to 1900 m. The southern portion of the park is primarily montane, and is characterized by forests of Douglas fir, white spruce, lodgepole pine and aspen. Under the trees, shrubs like buffaloberry, wild rose and juniper are commonly found. Bearberry (kinnikinnik) often covers the ground, usually accompanied by a variety of flowers and grasses.

This is the warmest and driest of the three ecoregions, and, consequently, it has an extensive history of forest fires. That accounts for the predominance of lodgepole pine in some areas. Their hard cones respond to sudden high temperatures and disperse thousands of heat-resistant seeds that germinate readily in the carbon-rich soil.

The greatest diversity of wildlife is found in this zone, including major populations of hooved mammals such as elk, white-tail deer and mule deer. Other large animals most often observed include coyotes, black bears and moose. Woodpeckers, ruffed grouse, ravens, juncos and chickadees are common

Prickly pear cactus is found in the southwest corner of the park. Photo Bob Hahn.

birds. This region also has the highest concentration of *Homo sapiens*.

The Subalpine

Most of Kootenay National Park is classed as subalpine. Above Kootenay Crossing, the montane zone is found only along the rivers (including the Simpson) to Vermilion Crossing. Beyond Vermilion Crossing you are primarily driving through the subalpine zone.

This zone ranges from the upper levels of the montane up to about 2300 m or wherever the trees end. Engelmann spruce and subalpine fir are the predominant tree species at the lower levels of the subalpine, often growing in dense stands. At higher elevations, the forest opens up and subalpine larches appear. Stunted trees are the norm as you go higher. These often grow as flattened, waist-high islands called *kruppelholz* (a German word for crippled trees). Again, where forest fires have interrupted normal growth patterns in the last 150 years, as in the Vermilion Pass Burn (1968), lodgepole pines can outnumber all the other species of trees.

Common shrubs are false azalea, grouseberry and alder. In season, patches of blooming heather brighten the ground under the trees. Of course, high meadows in full flower are an unforgettable highlight of this region.

The thick forest cover ensures that a deep layer of snow blankets the area during most of the long winter, making travel difficult. There are very few signs of animal life at that time. However, evidence of smaller mammals such as porcupines and snowshow hares might be seen. Bird life is also scarce, but no matter what the season, the raucous calls of Clark's nutcrackers and gray jays often interrupt the silence.

Aspens flourish in the montane zone. Photo Bob Hahn.

For most of the larger animals such as elk and grizzly bears, the subalpine is a zone of transition. They pass through either going up in the early summer or down in the fall. However, the region is critical for a trio of forest carnivores: marten, fisher and lynx.

The Alpine

From about 2300 m on up, the environment is the harshest in the park. Here, in the alpine zone, there are no trees, and the growth patterns of other plants are altered drastically. In this barren region, even willows hug the ground to escape the incessant winds. Mosses and lichens are found on the rocks. Other hardy flora include mountain avens, moss campion and western

Most of the park is subalpine including this scene of the Vermilion Pass Burn. Photo Bob Hahn.

The alpine region is beautiful but harsh. Photo Bob Hahn.

Opposite: Radium Hot Springs pool. This couple is sitting directly above the springs that supply hot water for the pool, now covered by concrete. Photo Bob Hahn.

golden-mantled ground squirrels, which can find shelter among the rocks, live here year-round. Rosy finches and pipits are often seen flitting about the barren slopes.

Of the larger mammals, grizzly bears, wolverines, bighorn sheep, mountain goats and mule deer range the high areas in summertime. Usually the goats are the only ones to brave the fierce winter weather and seek sustenance on windblown ridges, but wide-ranging wolverines may occasionally wander by the area.

Of course, variations in habitat occur in all three of the ecoregions. Individual ecological communities can range from dense forest to open grasslands, from arid slopes to marshes and riverbanks, from talus-covered mountainsides to fire-altered forests. Each mini-region has a unique community of plants and animals that are constantly changing. Keep your eyes open and listen carefully. You may observe something few visitors ever see.

anemone. Miniature versions of harebells, and some of the other flowers found at lower elevations can also be seen.

As you might imagine, the alpine area has the smallest number and variety of wildlife. Little creatures such as pikas, hoary marmots and

24

Radium Hot Springs Area

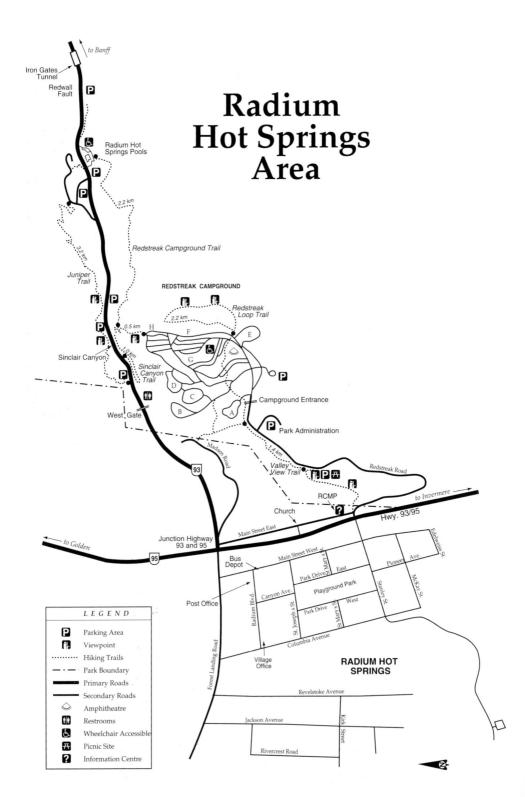

Radium Hot Springs Area

to Banff

Iron Gates Tunnel
Redwall Fault

Radium Hot Springs Pools

2.2 km

Redstreak Campground Trail

Juniper Trail

3.2 km

REDSTREAK CAMPGROUND

2.2 km

Redstreak Loop Trail

0.5 km

H   F   E

1.0 km   G

Sinclair Canyon

Sinclair Canyon Trail   D

West Gate   C

B   A

Campground Entrance

Park Administration

Madsen Road

93

1.4 km

Valley View Trail

Redstreak Road

to Invermere

RCMP

Church

Hwy. 93/95

Junction Highway 93 and 95

to Golden

95

Main Street East

Bus Depot

Main Street West

St. Mary's St.

Pioneer Ave.

Edelweiss St.

Park Drive   East

Post Office

Radium Blvd.

Canyon Ave.

St. Joseph's St.

Playground Park

Stanley St.

McKay St.

Park Drive   West

St. Mary's St.

Forest Landing Road

Columbia Avenue

Village Office

RADIUM HOT SPRINGS

Revelstoke Avenue

Jackson Avenue

Kirk Street

Rivercrest Road

N

LEGEND

P	Parking Area
	Viewpoint
········	Hiking Trails
—·—·—	Park Boundary
——	Primary Roads
—	Secondary Roads
	Amphitheatre
	Restrooms
	Wheelchair Accessible
	Picnic Site
	Information Centre

The Village of Radium Hot Springs

To reach the village of Radium Hot Springs, you have to negotiate some hills—downhill if you're coming from the south on Highway 93/95, or uphill if you're coming from the north on Highway 95. The only four-way stop in town is the junction of the two highways, and here is where the backseat driver should tell you to turn east. Located about 2 km up the road, around the corner from "motel row," is the entrance to the park.

Radium has a motel for every day of the month, and a couple extra for rainy days—when they are really needed. Yet, on a busy holiday weekend, finding a room isn't easy. Stop at the Visitor Information Centre as you come into town (see map) if you need help in finding a place to rest your weary head.

Numerous restaurants are located near the junction, serving everything from Chinese to German food. Fill up in town, because there isn't much to eat in the park except berries, and the bears have first rights. Actually, you can get some snacks at the hot pools, and there are also dining rooms at Radium

Hot Springs Lodge across from the pools and at Kootenay Park Lodge (Vermilion Crossing, km 63).

Motel owners in Radium Hot Springs try to outdo each other with lavish floral displays. Photo Bob Hahn.

Bighorn sheep gather in Radium as winter approaches. Photo John Pitcher.

27

Youngsters wait for the program to start at the Redstreak Amphitheatre.

Information, Please

"Can you tell me the location of any undiscovered lakes in the park?" "How high does a sheep have to get before it becomes a goat?" Those questions are a little tougher to answer than the ones usually asked of the staff at the park's information centres, but the friendly people behind the counter might surprise you with their knowledge. Their primary purpose is to give out information on the park, but ask almost any question and if they don't know the answer, they can probably put you in touch with somebody who does. (Sorry kids, that doesn't include homework.) If you're looking for information on the West Coast ferry system, the most scenic route to Alaska or a place to get your air mattress retreaded, you may find somebody on duty who knows the answer.

Here you can get park entry passes, fishing licences, visitor guides, maps, brochures, backcountry reservations and schedules of interpretive events. The latest weather report is usually posted as well as up-to-date news of trail conditions and bear sightings. You can also check on the availability of campground spaces—even in adjoining parks.

Too many travellers miss out on what the area has to offer because they don't take the time to talk to the people who know. Try to engage an attendant in conversation, if it isn't too crowded, and you might learn some surprising things—from the location of a little-known trail to where mountain ladyslippers are blooming. It's well worth a stop.

Visitor Information

The Visitor Centre is located at the south end of Radium Hot Springs Village (see map). It is housed in a stone building that used to be the RCMP headquarters. You can still contact the RCMP here, but the building is now used as a joint information centre by Parks Canada and British Columbia Tourism.

Friends of Kootenay National Park

Many parks in Canada and the USA are fortunate to have non-profit co-operating associations called Friends. The organization associated with Kootenay National Park was incorporated in 1995, making it one of the newest cooperating associations for Parks Canada. The Friends support education and research in the park.

Located in the Visitor Information Centre, the Friend's gift shop stocks maps, postcards, park-specific souvenirs and guidebooks like this one. Using the profits from the bookstore as well as grants, the Friends' are able to:

– help fund research in the park, i.e., wolves, lynx research
– sponsor free guided walks in the park for visitors
– organize "Take a Hike" and other events for Parks Day in July
– sponsor the Wild Voices speaker series (presentations on wildlife and wilderness in local communities)
– fund worthwhile projects including this book

It pays to have Friends!

A visit with one of the cheerful staff at the information centres is time well spent.

Where's Redstreak Campground?

The turnoff for Redstreak Campground is located next to the Visitor Centre. Follow the road 2 km up the hill past a parking area for the Valley View trail and the Administration Building. At the campground kiosk, a friendly attendant should offer greetings and help find just the type of campsite you are looking for. On rare occasions the kiosk may not be manned, but just follow the directions posted.

Redstreak is the largest and most developed campground in the park and the one most likely to be filled on a long weekend. Typical visitors are those who like their park experience combined with the amenities of civilization whether it's just a refreshing shower or a fine meal at some nearby restaurant. There are also many good short hikes in the area incuding an easy one to the Radium Hot Springs Pools.

Camping at Redstreak

Redstreak is the only serviced campground, with a total of 242 sites. Of this number, 50 are fully serviced (water, sewer and electricity), and 38 have electricity only. The remainder are unserviced. There are also 19 walk-in sites. There are playgrounds for the kids. This is the only campground that has showers and a public telephone. Interpretive programs are presented most nights of the week in an open amphitheatre. Check at the kiosk for a schedule. Redstreak opens in mid-May and is the last campground to close, usually in late September.

The following facilities are also available, in addition to those mentioned above:

wheelchair-accessible washrooms
kitchen shelters
sanitation stations
fireboxes
firewood
recycling bins
food storage for cyclists

Nearby Walks

See map on page 26 for trailhead locations and distances.

Valley View Trail

This easy, self-guiding trail winds through a forest of mostly Douglas fir right into the campground. It also connects with other paths to the village. By following the trail through the campground, you reach the amphitheatre. Check to see if any interpretive programs are scheduled. Just across the road, beyond the theatre, is the Redstreak Loop trail.

Redstreak Campground Trail

The Redstreak Campground trail is a pleasant forested walk with only the distant sounds of traffic in Sinclair Canyon to disturb you. Watch for the **Place of Silence**, Kootenay's own peace park. Take a seat among the towering red cedars, close your eyes and imagine how it must have felt to a lone aboriginal boy contemplating his future many years ago.

My most memorable wildlife sighting along this path had little to do with silence. It was a pileated woodpecker standing on the ground, whacking away at the base of huge Douglas fir, like some demented red-haired logger.

Located near the end of the trail is a good overview of the pool. The actual hot springs are not visible, but they are located at the base of the cliff nearest the highway. The trail leads you right to the "back door" of the pool area. Have an ice cream cone and a refreshing dip.

To return to the campground, there are three alternatives. Of course, one is to simply retrace your steps, but if you want to explore more of the park, try the **Juniper trail** (see page 37) on the

Hikers on the Juniper trail look down into Sinclair Canyon. Courtesy Kootenay National Park. Photo Marla Oliver.

other side of Sinclair Canyon. Your third choice is to stroll down the sidewalk that parallels the highway. In either case, the return to your starting point is via the 1 km **Sinclair Canyon trail** (see page 37).

The Place of Silence

Located about half a kilometre above the Radium Hot Springs Pools, in a grove of towering red cedars along the Redstreak Campground trail, is a plaque. It is dated December 15, 1992, and the heading reads, "The Place of Silence Peace Park." This special place is one of at least 385 peace parks across the country designed to create more public awareness of Canada's commitment to world peace and environmental protection.

Yet, long before Canada became a nation, this was a sacred place for aboriginal peoples. Boys on the verge of manhood came here as part of their vision quest, a period of fasting and meditation, seeking a sign from guardian spirits called "nipikas." Perhaps the wind, whispering through the trees, spoke to them. Whatever the message, it should have come through loud and clear, because back then, it was indeed the Place of Silence.

Yarrow (Achillea millefolium) was named after the Greek Achilles, who used it to staunch blood flow in wounded soldiers. Photo Gillean Daffern.

Redstreak Loop Trail

This 2.2 km loop is a good way to work up an appetite, while enjoying some grand views of the Columbia Valley and the Purcell Mountains beyond. Yes, the Purcells—many people assume all the mountains in view are part of the Rockies, but it isn't so. That's why any guided hike on this trail is usually advertised as "The Edge of the Rockies." The distant mountains are older, and have a different origin and composition (see page 144).

The division between the two mountain ranges is a geological phenomenon in itself. The **Rocky Mountain Trench** stretches from the U.S. border into the Yukon and is visible from outer space (see page 18).

The trail starts across the road from the theatre and climbs uphill through Douglas firs and juniper shrubs. Early in the summer yellow balsam root, pale violet beard-tongue, blue harebells, mariposa lily and other wildflowers bloom along the trail, but the dry climate discourages most blossoms later on.

There is an assortment of other interesting plants, but two stand out because of their names. The first is bearberry. The aboriginal peoples used to mix the mealy red bearberries with tastier berries and then added animal fat, ending up with a slow-spoiling food called pemmican. I've never tasted pemmican, and don't know if I want to, but I love the melodious native name for the bearberry plant: kinnikinnik. It's an Algonquin word for "tobacco substitute," indicating another use for the plant.

All living things have at least two names, a common one and a scientific one. Many European visitors recognize yarrow's flat-top clusters of tiny white flowers and fern-like leaves, but they call it by a different name. However, the scientific name is the same everywhere. Unfortunately, most people forget the longer Latin terms—yet they can be very descriptive. Yarrow is *Achillea millefolium*. If the genus, *Achillea,* reminds you of your Achilles tendon, it's because both are named after the same ancient Greek. It's reported that Achilles placed the crushed leaves of this plant on the wounds of soldiers to aid clotting. And it is a fact that they will help. However, remember not to pick any flowers in the park—just keep bleeding.

The trail leads to two excellent viewpoints, where you can rest on the benches provided and reflect on the incredible forces that created the scene before you. Also, look at the busy valley below and contemplate what might happen to the land you just passed through if it wasn't preserved in a national park. Linger awhile at the second viewpoint and watch the sunset. Once you leave, it's all downhill.

Watch for some huge fire-scarred firs near the bottom. Just beyond these survivors the trail forks, with the left path going back to where you started and the right dropping quickly to Loop F. From there you can follow the road back to the trailhead.

A Drive Through the Park

Entrance to Sinclair Canyon. Photo Bob Hahn.

Kootenay National Park

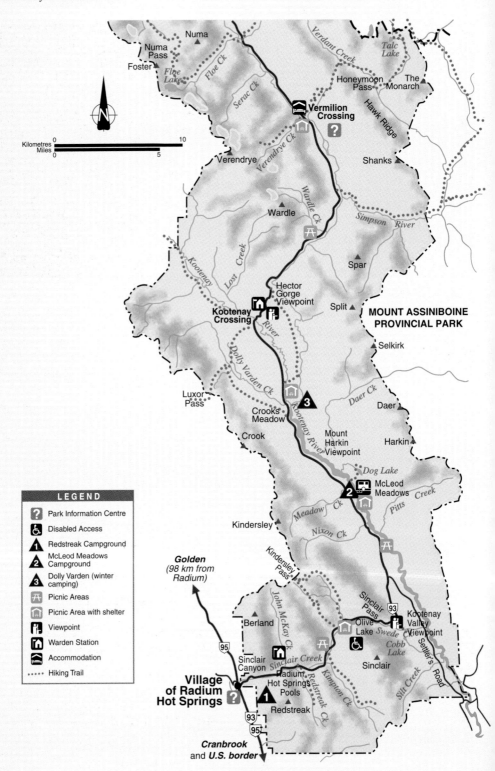

THE MOUNTAINS SHALL BRING PEACE TO THE PEOPLE

km 0 (94.5)

NOTE: The first kilometre distance is from the West Gate at the south end of the park, the second from the Great Divide at the north end.

West Gate Kiosk: Expect to pay a fee here for entrance to the park. Several types of passes, for varying lengths of time, are available, so figure out how long you expect to stay in Kootenay, Banff, Yoho and/or Jasper national parks. Passes are good for all four contiguous parks and there may be additional options. With over 20,000 km² in these parks, don't plan on seeing all the sights no matter how long you stay. Washrooms are located in the building to the right after you enter the gate.

Entrance fees

Entrance fees are required of anyone entering the park unless they are travelling straight through without a stop. Having a quick picnic, or stretching your legs on a short trail is considered a stop. Travelling the Icefields Parkway (Highway 93 north of Lake Louise), whether planning to stop or not, requires an entrance pass.

The fees go into a fund earmarked for park maintenance and improvements, and not just into general revenue. In Kootenay, among other things, they help pay for an information centre, a variety of exhibits, picnic areas, washrooms, numerous front country trails, several scenic viewpoints and regular garbage pick-ups.

The most logical time to purchase day or annual passes is when you enter the park, but this is only possible at the West Entrance. However, passes are good in all the Rocky Mountain parks, so anyone coming from the north should already have one. Passes can also be purchased at the Visitor Centre, the Radium Hot Springs Pools and at various outlets outside the park. There are discounts for groups or seniors. Prior to arrival, try to determine the length of your stay in the parks, in order to ascertain what pass will be most economical. All fees are subject to change, but current entrance fees are posted on the park's website (www.worldweb.com/ParksCanada-Kootenay).

Use of park attractions such as the hot pools or campgrounds is not covered by the entrance fee. Most interpretive programs are free, but there is a charge for others.

The village of Radium Hot Springs has no banks, but there is an automated teller machine at the Petro-Canada station. The last banking stop when coming from the south is Invermere; from the north, Golden. There is no place to change currency in Kootenay National Park.

This sign at the West Entrance emphasizes one of the most important reasons for the existence of national parks like Kootenay. Photo Bob Hahn.

What's the Weather Report?

It has been said only amateurs and fools try to predict weather in the Rocky Mountains. Thus, only neophytes venture very far from their vehicles without an assortment of clothing designed to withstand the changing elements. However, rest assured that snowshoes probably won't be required on a typical summer visit.

Here in the mountains, those very pinnacles are the major reason weather patterns can be so confusing. They act as a huge fence, impeding systems moving from west to east. In most cases the clouds have to "climb the fence," and may end up leaving some excess baggage behind in the form of precipitation. Thus Banff should logically be drier than the village of Radium Hot Springs. Yet, cacti are found near Radium! Confusing, yes, but look across the Columbia Valley and you'll see another mountain barrier: the Purcells. Radium is so close to the Purcell Mountains that it sits in their rain shadow.

Another big difference is changing altitudes. Along the highway in Kootenay National Park it ranges from 900 m at the West Gate to 1650 m at Vermilion Pass. With an increase in elevation, temperature usually decreases, and the cooler the air, the less moisture it can hold. Thus, as you gain elevation, you can expect more precipitation, more often, and more frequently in a solid form. In addition, hold on to your hat because the wind usually blows harder—but keep your head down, because chances of lightning strikes increase. If you get tired of hiking in that position, lie down and rest. Besides, it's warmer and calmer close to the ground. That's why most alpine plants are ground-huggers.

Kootenay National Park has a continental climate, which means brief, cool summers and long, snowy winters. The annual weather records bear this out.

Few people complain about too much sun, but only darn fools plan a vacation for rainy times. During the summer, count on rain about one day out of three in most areas of the park. However, chances decrease near the hot pools (1 out of 4) and increase at higher altitudes (1 out of 2). Keep in mind that this is an average, not a reliable pattern. Thus, with luck, you could enjoy a week or more of clear weather and leave your expected two or three days of drips with unsuspecting new arrivals.

Current weather reports are available at the information centres—but nothing is guaranteed.

Summer weather at the Radium Hot Pools (Elev. 1088 m)

Average Temperatures

	May	June	July	Aug.	Sept.	Oct.
High	18	20	23	21	16	10
Low	1	4	4	4	-2	-4

Average Number of Days With Rain

May	June	July	Aug.	Sept.	Oct.
9	10	8	8	8	6

km 0.2 (94.3)   **Juniper Trailhead (south):** Paved parking area on the left, just above the washrooms (not the gravel one just across the highway). A 10 minute walk downhill takes you into Sinclair Canyon and a beautiful waterfall on Sinclair Creek. This cool stop is a quick fix on a hot day, but the best way to do the entire 3.2 km Juniper route is to start at the other end (see page 39).

km 0.4 (94.1)   **Sinclair Canyon Trailhead:** A 1 km trail that begins on the right just before you enter the canyon. It switchbacks up to join the Redstreak Campground trail (see page 31). Turn left at the junction for the hot pools (2.2 km) and right to the campground (0.5 km).

km 0.5 (94.0)   **Sinclair Canyon:** This is probably the most spectacular entrance to any national park in Canada. However, before being widened to accommodate the highway, it was a forbidding place. Even aboriginal peoples avoided the dark narrow defile, and George Simpson (see page 12) called it a "...horrid gorge." Watch for parking areas on both sides of the highway, just beyond the entrance to the canyon. A short walk back allows you to see an excellent example of a thrust fault (see page 18). It's most obvious on the south side. There is also a viewing area on the other side of the road that almost gives a bird's-eye view of the waterfall on Sinclair Creek. To get a good view, hike down the Juniper trail.

No mountainous area is static. There is always the danger of falling rocks. In a narrow, heavily-travelled canyon such as Sinclair, errant boulders could easily mean tragedy. To avoid accidents, a rock-scaling crew is called in every few years to "encourage" unstable rocks and other debris to slide down while the highway is closed to traffic. If some of the cliffs look unusual to you, they may have been sprayed with concrete to stabilize them—and for your peace of mind.

Overnight Accommodations: The first road on your left takes you to the only accommodations in the park other than Kootenay Park Lodge (62 km). There are three sets of cabins to the left of the turn-off, while Radium Hot Springs Lodge is located near the end of the road. Just beyond the lodge is a picturesque stone building that was home for numerous park superintendents. It

Guided hikes are conducted on many of the trails near Radium Hot Springs. Courtesy Kootenay National Park. Photo Marla Oliver.

Bathers enjoy the soothing warmth of the Radium Hot Springs Pools year-round. Photo Bob Hahn.

The Radium Hot Springs Pools

One of the most commonly asked questions about the Radium Hot Springs Pools is, "Where does the hot water come from?" Some people believe the water coming out of the springs may have chilled them on a previous park visit when it fell from the sky. That might be partially true, but it's unlikely. Most of the water has come from so deep that it took thousands, if not millions, of years to get down there. But on the way up, the flow is diluted a bit with normal groundwater, which might be only tens of years old.

The deeper the water, the warmer it is. At depths of 3 km or more, the temperature is above 100°C, but the pressure down there keeps the water from boiling. Given an easy path to the surface, it will rise.

Water for the hot springs—there are actually four—rises along a natural conduit: the Redwall Fault. The fault provides a deep enough break in the rock layers to allow the hot water to move up. The same tremendous power that forced the red cliffs to stand on end also caused shattering of rocks (look across the highway from the hot pool, and you'll find no layering, only a jumble of rocks). The hot water easily finds a route up between the broken rocks.

As you might imagine, earthquakes can affect the flow from the hot springs. The huge Alaskan quake that occurred on March 27, 1964, muddied the water and caused the temperature of the hottest spring to drop from 45°C to 39°C. However, all was back to normal by April 7.

Disabled Access

Facilities at the Radium Hot Springs Pools allow virtually anyone access to the pools. They include:

- Four designated parking spots
- Ramp from parking lot to entrance
- Elevator
- Waterbug—a submersible wheelchair to take into the pools
- Two manual wheelchairs
- Hoyer lift (cool pool in summer only)
- Ramp (hot pool in summer only)
- Regular stairs into pools (no ladders)

---

has recently been converted to an office for pool personnel. At one time, a whole community existed in this area.

km 1.5 (93.0)   **Juniper Trailhead (north):** (3.2 km one way, elevation loss 200 m) Follow the route described in the preceding entry, and keep going uphill until you see a large, isolated boulder on your left. A small yellow sign tells you this is the spot. The 3.2 km trail follows the north rim of the canyon to spectacular views of the Columbia Valley and the mountains beyond. Warnings about cougars have occasionally been posted for this area, but there have never been any human injuries recorded.

These dry, open slopes are typical of benches above the Rocky Mountain Trench. Douglas fir, junipers and grasses predominate. Watch for light-coloured fur on the firs. Bighorn sheep frequent this area and when their winter coats start to itch—meaning it's time to shed—the rough bark of a Douglas fir provides an ideal scratching post. Watch for the sheep's tell-tale pellets on the ground. Be sure to tell the kids not to eat any "raisins."

km 1.6 (92.9)   **Radium Hot Springs Pools:** There are three parking lots for the pools. If you have a large motorhome or trailer, stop at the first lot on the left, no matter which direction you are travelling (see map page 34). Travellers coming from the north will find parking across from the Redwall Fault. There is an admission charge for the pools. Towels and bathing suits can be rented. Facilities include change rooms, showers and coin-operated lockers. Equipment is provided to accommodate disabled persons. If the hot water (40°C) isn't soothing enough, a massage service is also available.

The pools (one hot and one cool) are open year-round, but hours vary. Snacks and souvenirs can be purchased during the summer season. Bring your own food in the winter, but remember, it's considered bad etiquette to cook eggs in the pool.

Bathers of all ages enjoy the soothing waters of Radium Hot Springs.

The colour of the Redwall Fault—a break in the earth's crust—comes from hematite (oxidized iron). Photo Bob Hahn.

km 2.4 (92.1)   **Redwall Fault:** Around the curve above the pools you are suddenly dwarfed by a wall of red rock reminiscent of the southwestern U.S. desert country. Not only is the colour unusual—it comes from hematite (oxidized iron)—but the layer is on end. Tremendous pressure folded the rock upright until it finally broke (see page 18). Shattered rocks and finer particles were cemented together to form a concrete-like rock that geologists call breccia (BRETCH-yuh). The break, or fault, goes down several kilometres into the earth's crust. It extends north to Edgewater (10 km) and as far south as Canal Flats (50 km). Hot water rising along the fault supplies the springs. Bighorn sheep frequent the area because it supplies some basic needs: grass for food and escape terrain. The Redwall and other nearby cliffs enable the sheep to avoid either predatory coyotes or overzealous wildlife photographers.

km 2.4 (92.1)   **The First Campground:** In 1923, when construction of government buildings in the park began, work was also started on Red Rock Campground. As the name implies, the campground was near the Redwall Fault. Many of the old campsites are now covered by the asphalt of either the parking lot or the highway. You can still see remnants of the old road on the slope north of the present highway.

Obviously, there was no room for expansion of Red Rock Campground, and it steadily became more crowded and less satisfactory as visitation increased. The number of campers went from 93 in 1942 to 12,880 in 1962, the last year the campground was open. The number of campers registered the last year would have been twice as great if Redstreak Campground hadn't been opened to the public for the first time. Work on Redstreak continued until 1965, when it was completed.

Late afternoon light reflects from the Redwall Fault on Sinclair Creek. Photo Bob Hahn.

SPECIAL TREAT: Take your camera and follow the path along Sinclair Creek from the upper parking lot to the Hot Pools in the late afternoon. Look back at the creek and you'll see one of the lovelier sights in the park. The rushing water is turned to burnished gold by light reflected from the Redwall Fault.

Iron Gate Tunnel: km 2.5 (92.0) This tunnel was built in the mid-sixties in order to preserve the scenic values of the rocky ridge forming the "Iron Gate." Portions of the only remaining unaltered portion of Sinclair Canyon can be seen below the highway. Guided walks into this "secret canyon" are sometimes offered. To the north of the present highway you can see how the old road used to go over the top.

Meet a Tree

To some people, any tree with needles is a pine. And pines can be called evergreens, because they never lose their needles. If you believe those two statements, it's time to "leaf" off that way of thinking, branch out and get to the root of your problem.

It is correct to say that most of the needled conifers (cone-bearing trees) found in the Rocky Mountains belong to the pine family, but all the members aren't pines. Don't be confused. Grouping of other living things is similar. For instance, the weasel family does contain weasels, but wolverines, martens and fishers are also members. Thus, in addition to pines, the pine family also includes spruce, firs and larches.

Without getting too scientific, it's fairly easy to differentiate between conifers just by examining their

Top: Lodgepole pine needles. Courtesy Kootenay National Park. Photo Larry Halverson. Middle: Fir needles. Photo Gillean Daffern. Bottom: Spruce needles and cone. Photo Gillean Daffern.

needles. Pine needles are the longest, and are the only ones arranged in bundles (2-5 in the Canadian Rocky Mountains). The needles of spruce are much shorter, stiff and sharp (squeeze a branch). They are four-sided and can easily be rolled between your fingers. Fir needles are soft, flat and don't want to be rolled. The needles of larches are soft and grow from little bumps on the branches, like hairs on a wart.

Most people aren't likely to find a larch in Kootenay Park unless they hike up to treeline, where subalpine (Lyall's) larches occur. However, there are a few western larches along the highway, near the Kootenay Valley viewpoint (see page 51) and farther south.

Despite the needles and cones, larches are not evergreens. The needles turn yellow and gold in the fall and eventually fall to the ground. It should be obvious that the evergreens also lose their needles, but not all at the same time. Just look at the ground under a Douglas fir. There are often so many needles that growth of other plants is greatly hindered—owing more to excess acidity than the depth of the duff.

People like me, who love the natural world, have often been referred to as tree huggers, but you don't have to get that intimate to know a tree. Look at the needles, and if they're short (eliminating pines), squeeze a bunch with your hand. You can even do it with your eyes closed. If you say "Ouch!" it's a Sharp Spruce; if not, you've just met a Friendly Fir. If it growls, you don't have a tree at all. Good luck.

For easy reference, just remember this about the needles:
Pine: long (2-20 cm) and in bundles
Spruce: short, sharp, four-sided
Fir or Douglas fir: short, soft, flat

After a short scramble above the Kindersley-Sinclair Col, it appears the whole world consists of mountains. Photo Bob Hahn.

km 3.9 (90.6) **Maintenance Compound:** The fenced area on the left is the heart of the park apparatus because this is where supplies are stored and all the machinery for road work comes to rest. It's also where the mechanics practise their monkey-wrenching magic, carpenters hammer out decisions, painters work on perfecting their strokes, electricians come to shocking conclusions and the trail crew sharpens their chainsaws. A short road continues beyond the compound to the McKay Creek Operations Centre, containing warden headquarters and offices for the park interpreters and other personnel.

km 4.5 (90.0) **Redstreak Creek Trailhead:** (2 km one way, elevation gain 90 m) Watch for a small roadside pull-off on the south side of the highway. Cross Sinclair Creek on a footbridge and follow the pleasant forested trail along the creek to the trail's-end sign.

km 7.3 (87.2) **Kimpton Creek Trailhead:** (5 km one way, elevation gain 340 m) Parking for this trail is just beyond the trailhead. Walk back along the south side of the highway to another footbridge across the creek and follow Kimpton Creek into a forested canyon. This trail is similar to Redstreak, but goes farther before fizzling out. It's a cool shaded walk for a hot day.

km 9.0 (85.5) **Sinclair Creek Picnic Area:** North side of the highway. Toilets, water and a dozen tables for your outdoor dining pleasure.

km 9.5 (85.0) **Kindersley Pass Trailhead:** (10.1 km to Kindersley-Sinclair Col, elevation gain 1055 m) Parking is on the south side of the highway. Cross carefully to find the trail. This trail offers a longer but more gentle route to the Kindersley-Sinclair Col than the Sinclair Creek trail. It is primarily a forested route so alpine vistas are not readily apparent for most of the hike. In early summer watch carefully along the initial reaches for rare mountain lady's-slippers.

Who's Coming for Dinner?

A pair of Clark's nutcrackers waiting for handouts. Resist the urge to feed these dinner guests. Photo Bob Hahn.

Just as you're sitting down to enjoy a picnic lunch in one of Kootenay's quiet roadside stops, a flutter of wings announces the arrival of visitors. Three plump birds with smoky-gray bodies and paler heads watch from nearby trees as you spread out the goodies. You can easily imagine them saying, "What's for lunch?" Ever the opportunist, the gray jay (an older name is Canada jay) is willing to sample anything, from your peanut butter sandwich to Grandma's homemade dill pickles. In fact, if you don't keep an eye on the food, the jays are likely to live up to their other common label of camp robber.

The same moniker is also applied to another family member often mistaken for the gray jay that has similar habits. However, Clark's nutcrackers are easy to distinguish with their longer black beaks and flashy black and white wings. They are a little larger than Canada jays and much noisier—especially in late spring, when the young follow mom and dad around, screaming harshly for more to eat. In some of the subalpine campgrounds of Banff and Jasper, the "Kraw! Kraw!" lasts from sunrise to sunset.

Resident gray jays are present at most picnic areas and campgrounds. Photo Gillean Daffern.

Whereas Clark's nutcrackers are flamboyant, gray jays give the impression of quiet, twinkling-eyed uncles. Oh, they can be noisy, too, and you never know what sounds are going to come out of their beaks. While hiking, I've sometimes been entranced by a mysterious, melodious song—an amazing bird symphony—only to discover its source was a single gray jay.

Both birds are very intelligent. Far from being bird brains, their memories are phenomenal. They frequently stash picnic leftovers and a wide variety of other foods for winter use. Gray jays actually use saliva to stick some of their hoard to the branches of trees. The Clark's nutcrackers hide food (their favourite snack is whitebark pine seeds) under tree bark or even in the ground, like squirrels. However, squirrels are absent-minded professors when it comes to finding any of their supplies. In contrast, both species of jays remember which "cupboards" to look in—and there can be thousands!

The Cree word for these jays is wiskatjon, which early settlers soon converted to whiskey-john and finally to whiskey-jack. But no matter what you call them, and no matter how far you wander from the beaten paths, when it's time to eat, look around. You never know who's coming for dinner.

Each exhibit at the Olive Lake picnic site has a tactile feature including this bronze replica of one of the small resident brook trout. Photo Bob Hahn.

If the distance doesn't faze you, the altitude gain might. However, the trail is excellent, with few steep spots, and the magnificent vista that unfolds in the distance acts as a magnet to draw you up the most difficult grades.

The path initially follows the rushing water of Sinclair Creek through a lush forest dominated by Douglas fir. Watch for calypso orchids and one-flowered wintergreen (single delight) in early summer. Higher up, avalanche slopes are covered by brilliant yellow glacier lilies.

This is grizzly bear country and bear warnings are sometimes posted. Don't ignore them. However, don't let the slight possibility of a bear encounter prevent you from experiencing the pleasures of this memorable trek. Just be sure to follow the suggestions for travelling in bear country on page 46.

A large snowpatch is often encountered by early season hikers just below the col. Follow the markers leading to the left. The trail to the right was designed by bighorn sheep who frequent the open ridges.

Scrambling either to the north or south from the col (2375 m) will give hikers unparalleled views of a sea of mountain peaks from the Bugaboos in the west to Mount Assiniboine in the east. Follow the trail along the ridge to Kindersley Pass and the route back to the highway.

km 11.9 (82.6) **Sinclair Pass Summit (1486 m) and the Olive Lake Picnic Area:** STOP! This is not just an ordinary picnic site. Long before national parks were even imagined, Olive Lake was a natural stopping point for people traversing Sinclair Pass. Artifacts discovered here indicate aboriginal peoples

Opposite: Use common sense in bear country and even long-clawed grizzlies like this will rarely cause problems.

47

Weasel Tag and Other Olive Surprises

Olive Lake is not considered to be a prime wildlife viewing area. Yet, in the past, as the displays indicate, bears often visited the area to strip bark from the trees and nibble on the then exposed cambium layer—where conducting vessels for the sweet sap are located. One black bear came here so often she was named after the lake. Quite frequently, Olive showed up in the spring with a pair of cubs, to the delight of visitors. Luckily, there were no bad incidents, but bears who aren't afraid of humans should never be taken lightly.

One afternoon a large black bear was frightened away from the road where it had been feeding and approached a group I was guiding. My excited companions forgot to surround the guide as they had facetiously been advised earlier, but I forgave them. It was a memorable experience, but not one I'd care to repeat.

Bears aren't the only animals that like Olive Lake. Some of my most interesting encounters have been with a variety of other critters—including one animal that we never actually saw. That happened one fall day when a couple of my cohorts and I stopped to check on revisions to the picnic area. That evening Larry Halverson, Chief Park Naturalist at that time, got a call.

"What did you think of the cougar?"

"What cougar?" responded a bewildered Larry.

"Why, the one that was sitting on the slope just across the highway from the picnic area watching you men!"

Never did we dream that we were the subject of a curious cat's close scrutiny.

But in late August of 1967, a cougar did more than look. At that time, it was possible to camp at Olive Lake. One evening, a cougar snatched a toy poodle from some California campers. Two evenings later, the cougar leaped out of the bush and grabbed a Calgary woman's 11 kg Irish terrier, ripping the leash right out of her hands.

A week or two later, on September 6, three maintenance crew members were working at the campground, and noticed a cougar watching them from the brush about 5 m away. They called a warden, who appeared within minutes and shot the animal. The cat was a healthy two year-old, a cougar "teenager," who thought he had found his happy hunting grounds—and, unfortunately, that's where he ended up.

Most of the hunters found in the Olive Lake area are no danger to either people or their pets. In fact, I enjoyed photographing a very serious huntress one September. It was a female coyote using all of her keen senses to locate supper. I silently cheered her on each time she leaped into the air and pounced on what she hoped was some unsuspecting rodent hidden in the grass.

Probably the rarest viewing pleasure I ever had at Olive occurred at the lake's outlet. My wife and I came upon a family of weasels playing "weasel tag," over and under the bridge. Occasionally, one of the fearless little sausage-shaped creatures stopped to give us the once-over, but they didn't stand still very long.

So—do as travellers have done for hundreds of years: make a stop at Olive Lake to enjoy the peace and serenity. Check out the exhibits, and eat your lunch.

Naturalist Glenys Snow (left), shown here with a group of visitors, was instrumental in designing the Olive Lake site. Photo John Pitcher.

camped by the lake as long ago as 11,000 years. It was only natural for the site to become a park campground, and finally, a picnic area.

However, in 1993 a major renovation was completed that puts Olive Lake in a class by itself. This area is completely accessible to people with disabilities, right down to the special exhibits. Elsewhere, few exhibits have anything for the visually handicapped. Here, besides supplying interesting information, each exhibit has a tactile feature. For example, bronzed replicas of tree bark make it possible for a blind person to identify different tree species in the area.

Other accessible features include widened paths to accommodate wheelchairs, and picnic tables that have been converted for those same wheelchair users. There are even two platforms built over the lake, accessible to all, where sightings of colourful brook trout are possible. One platform has an exhibit that includes a life-size bronze replica of one of the typically tiny trout found in the lake.

Shortly after the upgrading was completed, the area received a well-deserved national award. Pause, take a look and enjoy a sandwich. Maybe some of the soothing magic of Olive Lake's clear tranquil waters will work its wonders on you, just as it's done for other travellers for as long as we know.

Disabled Access

Kootenay National Park has made great strides in recognizing the needs of those visitors who have disabilities. The special-needs showplace of the park is Olive Lake with its uniquely designed exhibits and wheelchair access, but there are many other areas where modifications have been provided for the disabled.

Beetlemania

The above term could be applied to the reaction of foresters when mountain pine beetles invade prime stands of timber. In fact, it could even apply to the tiny beetles themselves, as they frantically burrow through the bark to lay eggs.

Evidence of the beetles' handiwork becomes most obvious when the pine needles die and turn reddish brown. But even before the tree dies, an examination of the bark may indicate the presence of the tree's nemesis. Look for small weeping wounds—dribbles of pitch. Pines attempt to fight off a beetle attack by producing enough pitch to flush them out the way they came in. Younger trees are generally successful in this pitching out. Trees over 80 years old usually succumb.

Another obvious sign that a tree is under siege from beetles is blue wood. The colour doesn't come directly from the insects, but from a fungus they carry. The fungus grows and clogs up the tree's water conducting system, while the beetle larvae girdle the tree by burrowing. This cuts off any supply lines and the tree dies.

The results of the double-pronged attack are not pretty. Yet the death of trees by beetles is as natural as death by forest fire (see page 70). Both cause a change in the age structure of the forest, and, in turn, an alteration in the types of organisms that live there. However, fires have been suppressed so long in the park—a policy that is changing—that there are more older trees than normal. More mature trees, more beetle-killed timber. Thus, in either case, nature ensures new life—and its consequent bio–diversity—through death. I kind of like the results of Ma Nature's handiwork.

The Mitchell Range rises above a fog-shrouded Kootenay River valley. Photo Bob Hahn.

Mount Sinclair is veiled in early morning clouds. Photo Bob Hahn.

km 14.6 (79.9)   **Cobb Lake Trailhead:** (2.8 km one way, elevation loss 190 m) This is a short forested walk to a pleasant, boggy lake. The trail goes downhill about 1.5 km to cross Swede Creek before climbing slightly to the lake. Note some of the huge fire-scarred Douglas firs. Their thick, deeply furrowed bark has enabled them to withstand the searing heat of forest fires that have killed other species. The lake reportedly contains some good-sized, but rarely caught, brook trout.

km 15.2 (79.3)   **Kootenay Valley Viewpoint:** Before you stretches an incredible vista. The milky-green waters of the Kootenay River can be seen far below as it snakes southward through a forest of evergreens. Across the valley, the Mitchell Range stretches to the sky. To the right is the Cross River valley, named for the wooden crucifix that Father de Smet planted in its upper reaches in 1845 (see page 13). Beyond the valley are the far distant peaks of Height of the Rockies Provincial Park.

Looking upstream, you'll note an abundance of beetle-killed pines on the lower slopes of the mountains. The loss of these trees is as natural as wolves killing elk and there is a definite similarity. You wouldn't ordinarily think of pine beetles as predators, but they do bore into living trees and eventually cause the pines to die. The exhibit tells you more.

Far beyond the dead trees (about 20 km) is a prominent gap between the Mitchell Range and the Vermilion Range. The highway passes through this cleft to connect the Vermilion and Kootenay river drainages.

Don't overlook the friendly creatures nearby. Tiny chipmunks (note the facial stripes and erect tail) usually vie with noisy, blue-crested Stellar's jays (the official British Columbia bird), and gray jays for handouts.

One year some well-meaning tourists caused a brief flurry of excitement with an unusual "wildlife sighting" at the viewpoint. They notified the Warden's Office that a man was peddling furs in the parking area. Wardens were racing from both ends of the park when an alert member of the highway crew radioed to tell them the exhibit was legitimate. As a park naturalist, I had set up a special display of park wildlife. It gave visitors a chance to see and handle horns, antlers and skins, but nothing was for sale. Any sale of animal parts in the park is illegal and might be suspect elsewhere.

Hikers take a breather below Sylvan Pass. Photo Bob Hahn.

park can be accessed by five other roads (in summer) that lead to its boundary. Travel beyond is restricted to hikers or horse traffic. No motorized vehicles are allowed, including float planes.

Boosters of this area claim there are more mountain goats in Height of the Rockies than anywhere in the world, which might be true. Other abundant species of large mammals include deer, elk and bears. Numerous lakes and streams beckon to anglers. The lure of trophy-size cutthroat trout prompts fishermen to puff and sweat on some of the steep trails. (Too often Forest Service routes follow old trails that used the "shortest distance between two points is a straight line" rule. Modern Forest Service designers do much better.)

A Height of the Rockies Provincial Park map and brochure can be picked up at the Forest Service office in Invermere. Topographic maps are available at the government agent's office next door.

Height of the Rockies

This 68,000 ha provincial park was previously the first designated B.C. Forest Service wilderness area. Like many other national and provincial parks, it is a region of high peaks, lush valleys and other natural wonders. There are 26 mountain peaks with summits over 3000 m in elevation, topped by Mount Joffre at 3449 m. In addition to Settler's Road, the

Solitude, plentiful cutthroat trout and reflections of Mount Queen Mary are powerful incentives to visit Ralph Lake. Photo Bob Hahn.

Photo Bob Hahn.

Western Larches: Shortly after you start downhill into the Kootenay River valley, if you are coming from the Radium end, watch for western larches on the river side of the highway. They're hard to distinguish from other conifers in the summer, but look for tall, somewhat scragglier looking trees. There is no problem locating them in the late fall, though. Their small needles change to a golden hue, then fall off. Kootenay is the only one of the four contiguous mountain parks to contain any specimens of western larch, even though the trees are very common in the southern portion of the Rocky Mountain Trench. A high altitude relative, subalpine larch (Lyall's larch), is fairly common in all the parks except Jasper.

km 19.0 (75.5)   **Settler's Road:** Does that name conjure up images of wagon trains, cowboys and buffalo? There was a shortage of all three in this part of the Rockies, but a few settlers did claim land in the Kootenay River valley, thus the name of the road—the first into the valley.

The distance from the junction of this gravel road with Highway 93 to the park boundary is 11 km. Trucks hauling magnesite (used for, among other things, magnesia, and heat-resistant materials such as fire brick) from the Baymag Mine are frequent travellers. The road is also used by rafters and canoeists to reach put-in and take-out points on the Kootenay River. This is the route to the Height of the Rockies Provincial Park and other wild destinations.

km 19.7 (74.8)   **Animal Lick:** Watch for a few patches of muddy ground on the east side of the highway, about a kilometre north of Settler's Road. There are no signs indicating the lick. Occasionally, a deer or moose can be seen slurping sulphur-rich minerals from the soggy ground. I've probably seen more

53

The Mitchell Range is reflected in the still waters of Dog Lake. Photo Bob Hahn.

and moisture-loving types of vegetation as you descend to the lake.

Four different species of wintergreen, so named because the leaves are green year-round, may be found along the trail. Don't expect the usual strong odor associated with the ointment for aching muscles. Oil of wintergreen comes from a different plant found in the eastern part of the continent. My favourite wintergreen has the charming label of single delight, because of the lovely, lone flower nodding from the short stem. Names for the wintergreens are simple and descriptive: single delight is also called one-flowered wintergreen; one-sided wintergreen has all its white flowers on the same side; green pyrola has green flowers, and the showiest of all, pink pyrola, has—you guessed it—about a dozen nodding pink flowers.

Once you reach the lake, you may be disappointed to discover more reeds than water, evidence of a shrinking lake. To reach the open water, continue along the trail for a short distance until another path leads to the right across a rustic bridge. This unmaintained, muddy route leads to the lake's east shore.

The Mitchell Range rises majestically beyond the lake. However, your desire to photograph may be tempered by the abundance of reddish-brown, beetle-killed pine trees (see page 50) on the slopes.

By continuing down the trail, which now follows the outlet of the lake, you will eventually reach the fireroad again. On one June excursion we found an incredible number of delicate calypso orchids in a single bed near the stream.

Turn left on the fireroad, and watch for the junction with the trail back to the river. Total round-trip distance is about 6 km.

Hike to Dog Lake

The hike to Dog Lake begins in either the McLeod Meadows picnic area or campground (across from the theatre). Kids love the initial part, as they stomp across the wiggling suspension bridge to an island in the Kootenay River. The riverbank on both sides of the bridge is good habitat for orchids (see page 68) and other wildflowers. Another bridge allows hikers to reach the far shore.

After a bit of a grunt up the hill, with excellent views back at the Brisco Range to the west, the trail crosses the East Kootenay fireroad.

Beyond the fireroad, the trail leads through montane forest with perhaps more varieties of tree species than can be seen anywhere in the park. It's an area that begins with an undergrowth of grasses, bearberry and other dry-environment plants—look for showy orange western wood lilies—and ends with mostly lichens, mosses

This peaceful scene should aid the digestion of any visitor to the Kootenay River picnic site. Photo Bob Hahn.

moose cows with gawky calves in this area than in any other part of the park. Keep to posted speed limits so that you don't miss wildlife sightings but you **do** miss wildlife that wanders onto the highway. I witnessed a near-collision here one evening between a little red sports car and a large bull moose. The moose literally escaped by a hair, but I'm afraid the people in the sports car would have fared the worst.

km 22.9 (71.6) **Kootenay River Picnic Site:** A great view and tables right on the bank of the Kootenay River make this a popular stop. It's also the last convenient take-out point for canoeists before they float out of the park, but the eddy has to be hit just right.

km 26.5 (68.0) **McLeod Meadows Picnic Area:** The wooded picnic area is separated from the campground by the meadow that gives this area its name. The open area often sports a yellow dressing of shrubby cinquefoil (meaning five leaves, but the flowers have five petals also) through much of the summer. There is an excellent view of the Brisco Range to the west. A good 2.6 km trail leads into the campground, past the rarely-used theatre, and on to Dog Lake.

Food always tastes better when cooked outdoors. Photo Bob Hahn.

A shelter, complete with wood stove, makes this a good lunch stop in rainy weather.

55

The Accidental Salmon

Once upon a time, long, long ago, before humans in their infinite wisdom decided to destroy the natural flow of the great Columbia River with dams, Kootenay National Park had a salmon run. Chinook (spring) salmon came up lower Sinclair Creek as far as the falls, where they were caught by the aboriginal peoples. But the dams came and the salmon went, never to return.

Then, in the fall of 1983, an amazing thing happened. Salmon showed up in the Kootenay River—not huge chinooks, but hundreds of trout-sized kokanee (landlocked sockeye salmon), dressed in Christmas colours of red and green. To the amazement of park officials, they crowded the gravel flats.

This unusual spectacle was the result of an accidental spill of kokanee fry in the Bull River near Cranbrook, about 85 km south of Radium Hot Springs. The fry went downstream into the Kootenay River and eventually to Koo–canusa Reservoir, which straddles the Canada-U.S. border. They flourished in the nutrient-rich new reservoir and after three years the 30-40 cm-long fish followed the call of their hormones to new spawning beds.

Too often the introduction of a new species has had less than wonderous results—the rabbit in Australia, the starling in North America. Yet, it's been nearly two decades for kokanee in the Kootenay (it even sounds poetic, doesn't it?) and no adverse effects to the environment have been noted. On the plus side, after the spawned-out salmon die, as they all do, they provide food for a variety of scavengers, especially bald eagles. And nutrients from the dead fish might make it possible for the upper river to support greater populations of cutthroat trout and other desirable species. It's all speculation, but whatever the results, it looks like the kokanee are here to stay.

Kokanee salmon are relative newcomers in the park. Courtesy Kootenay National Park. Photo Larry Halverson.

Camping at McLeod

McLeod has 98 unserviced (no hookups) campsites, and is probably the least used of the park's three drive-in campgrounds. Self-registration is required with all pertinent information being found in the little kiosk at the park entrance. Before planning to camp at McLeod, it is a good idea to check on fees, because there is no way to obtain change at the campground. There are no permanent attendants on duty, but there may be camp hosts on hand to answer questions. Even if you don't have any problems, take the time to meet the camp hosts. These volunteers know how to make anyone feel welcome.

McLeod is usually open from mid-May to mid-September.

Facilities at McLeod include:
piped water
kitchen shelters
fireboxes & firewood
wheelchair-accessible washrooms
recycling bins
food storage for cyclists

Campers at McLeod Meadows enjoy a sunny afternoon along the Kootenay River. Photo Bob Hahn.

km 26.9 (67.6)   **McLeod Meadows Campground:** For some reason, McLeod seems to be one of the hidden jewels of Kootenay Park, even though no one tries to keep it a secret. We often direct people to this quiet camp on the banks of the Kootenay River, but the campground is rarely filled to capacity.

At least four different kinds of orchids, beautiful shooting stars and lovely pink bird's-eye primrose make early season jaunts in this area a favourite of mine.

Come fall, the attractions are larger and louder, but less colourful. I'm referring to elk, who respond to ancient mating urges and begin to gather in the meadows. Of course, these large deer aren't stationary like plants, and can be difficult to locate, but listen carefully. If you are fortunate enough to hear a mature elk bugle, you'll never forget it—especially if it happens in the eerie pre-dawn gloom of a foggy morning. Even if the weather is warm, you'll probably experience a momentary shiver.

Bears have frequented the campground area in the past, but are rare visitors now. Some trees show signs of their visits. Look for scars left by a climbing bruin's claws on the powdery bark of an aspen. Also, check out any conifer with the lower bark stripped away—and often left hanging in shreds. The vertical marks are the teethmarks of a bear with a sweet tooth, who scraped away the cambium layer just like those at Olive Lake (see page 47).

It's a wonder more of those hungry bears haven't discovered the brightly coloured kokanee salmon that can often be spotted in the autumn from one of the two bridges over the Kootenay River. Historically, fish as a food source for bears is almost unheard of in the park. Yet, you'd think the keen-nosed bruins would be drawn to the stench of dead and decaying salmon faster than moths are drawn to a light. And it wouldn't take long for movement in the water to trigger hunting instincts. The bruin who accidentally discovers the red and green fish will have it all to himself—except for eagles and other birds that already dine on salmon.

57

Canoeists on the lower Kootenay. Photo Bob Hahn.

Running the Rivers

The only easily reached waters suitable for boating in the park are the Kootenay and Vermilion rivers. The Kootenay, below Hector Gorge, is an excellent choice for canoeists or kayakers with moderate skills, as it has relatively few rapids and these are no more than Class II for waters inside the park (there are class III rapids on Kootenay River outside the park along Settler's Road). The best access point is about 5 km north of McLeod Meadows, where the highway comes close to the river. Possible takeout points are McLeod Meadows Campground or the Kootenay River picnic area. The Columbia River between Invermere and Golden is perfect for novice paddlers.

Only experienced canoeists should put-in at the access about 2.5 km above the Hector Gorge viewpoint, because the canyon run can be hazardous. Some of the rapids are rated class IV at medium-to-high water levels. Use the take-outs mentioned above or continue south of the park with access off Settler's Road.

It is possible to rent canoes in Invermere. In addition a number of companies run canoe and raft trips on the Kootenay, Columbia and other nearby rivers. Ask at the Information Centre.

Yellowstone to the Yukon

The predicted problems in the transition to Y2K didn't materialize, but we are still faced with the difficulties in trying to establish the sound-alike Y2Y—a network of protected areas and connecting corridors that stretch all the way from the Yellowstone Plateau to the Yukon Highlands, a distance of almost 2000 miles.

Research has shown that animals such as wolves and grizzly bears roam great distances in search of food, quiet denning areas and proper mates—it's not wise for bears to breed with close relatives. These large carnivores need safe corridors for this travel and that is often impossible, even in our national parks. Most female grizzlies in Banff National Park refuse to cross the Trans-Canada Highway. Lynx in Kootenay and Yoho will rarely cross any highway.

The national parks are just not large enough to protect wide-ranging wildlife. That's why over 200 organizations on both sides of the border are working together to make the Yellowstone to Yukon Conservation Initiative become a reality. The survival of many of our large carnivores could depend on just how successful they are.

Cyclists Note: This is the first chance for northbound two-wheelers to get away from the highway if you have a mountain bike. You can pedal to the beginning of the Dog Lake trail, then walk your bike up to the East Kootenay fireroad. It used to be possible to cycle to a junction with the highway again north of Kootenay Crossing, but the Daer Creek bridge is now gone. It's also possible to have an additional adventure by following the fireroad south to a bridge across Pitts Creek. Leave your bike and take an unmaintained trail, which eventually peters out, up the west side of the creek. This is for experienced hikers only.

km 28.2 (66.3) **Mount Harkin Viewpoint:** Mount Harkin (2983 m) The highest mountain in the Mitchell Range is named after James B. Harkin, the first commissioner of national parks (1911-36). Harkin believed in the value of wilderness for its own sake, and worked to preserve spectacular parks such as Kootenay. He helped establish 11 other national parks, and his far-reaching visions and ideals have earned him the unofficial title of "Father of Canadian National Parks." Without his efforts, we would be a poorer nation by far.

59

Char have light spots on a dark background, just the opposite of other trout. Photo Bob Hahn.

Hello, Dolly! So Long, Dolly!

At one time anglers sought Dolly Varden char (a type of fine-scaled trout) in Kootenay National Park. Thus, we have the legacy of Dolly Varden picnic area and Dolly Varden Creek.

However, a few years ago some ichthyologists (people who study fish) decided the fishers weren't really catching Dolly Vardens at all. They said that real Dollys are found only along the West Coast, and that our fish are bull trout. South of us in Montana, folks have long talked about bull trout, but only because some of these Dolly Varden impersonators grow as big as bulls.

No matter what you call them, the fish are in trouble. Populations have declined to such an extent that it's illegal to keep any in many areas including the park.

Dolly Vardens have had a tough go of it over the years. With their huge mouths and voracious appetites, they have been blamed for decimating trout and salmon populations. Certainly, they are far from being vegetarians, but almost any large game fish prefers steak to salads. Yet, there was a 20-year-period in Alaska when bounties were paid for the tail of any dead Dolly. It became common to place the dried

tails on metal rings for later reimbursement. The rings even served as legal tender for many a poker game. Ironically, this well-meaning but faulty attempt to protect trout and salmon stocks backfired. Most of the officials who dished out bounty money couldn't tell the tail of a Dolly Varden from that of a prime salmon. Thus, the poker stakes were often higher than most anybody realized.

The name Dolly Varden comes from a flamboyantly dressed female character in Charles Dickens' book, *Barnaby Rudge*. Undoubtedly, the individual who christened the char saw them at their brightest—during fall spawning. Flanks take on a flaming colour, and bellies are red.

Anyway, this is all academic now, as we officially have only bull trout in the park, and few of them. Let's hope that by following the zero catch limit, numbers of bull trout will increase. If you fish, take the time to become familiar with the different species, and if there is any possibility at all that your catch is a bull trout, please release it unharmed. It's an integral part of your national park (see page 129).

Crooks Meadow Campground

Crooks Meadow is open year-round for group camping, and has a capacity of 75 people. The campground has a roomy shelter, with wood stove, abundant picnic tables, bearproof food storage, garbage containers and nearby water pump. The area also has a large playing field and a special fire circle with a good supply of wood. Washrooms are conveniently located near all the other facilities.

There is a minimum fee charged per person. Call the administration building, 250-347-9615, to make reservations.

km 31.1 (63.4)   **Kootenay Heart:** Watch for a large open flat on the east side of the high-way, a little over a kilometre beyond the Harkin Monument. Pull over to the side and look to the wide gap in the far mountains. Follow the treeline to the left past the first peak (Mount Selkirk) and drop your sight just a little. You should then be looking at the Kootenay Heart, in the heart of Kootenay Park. It's easy to miss, but once you see it, there's no mistaking it. This is a good place to bring your sweetheart on Valentine's Day. The heart is a natural formation.

The Goodsirs: The high peaks that you view straight down the highway are the twin towers of Mount Goodsir. The south tower at 3562 m is the highest point in Yoho National Park.

km 34.1 (60.4)   **Crooks Meadow Group Campground:** Site of an old homestead, this area must be reserved in advance.

Campers may also visit the grave of Charles Crook who owned the property until 1956 (see page 62).

km 35.7 (58.8)   **Dolly Varden Picnic Area:** Dolly Varden is the only area open to campers in the wintertime, and at the beginning of the 21st century it's still free. Compassionate park officials think camping in cold weather can be miserable enough without having to pay for it. The area is used mainly by visitors with RVs as there are no real campsites. Camping is permitted only after McLeod Meadows Campground closes in mid-September. In addition to the regular facilities, there are two shelters with wood stoves and a special display.

The Kootenay Heart in the heart of Kootenay Park. Photo Bob Hahn.

The picnic area and nearby creek are named after a fish once thought to swim in park waters—but biologists changed their minds. A hike up Dolly Varden Creek can take you to some decent fly fishing, and, as the rule goes, the farther you go, the less competition.

The Crook homestead was one of the earliest along the Kootenay River.

Cabins Along the Kootenay

You may have already passed Settler's Road (unless you're travelling south), where some pioneers built homes, but others squatted in what is now Kootenay Park.

Most well known is the Crook homestead, because the meadows there have been developed as a group campsite. Charles Crook claimed the property in 1911, but didn't "prove up" until about 1920. What he had to do to acquire title isn't known for sure. It might have involved just establishing residence on the land for a certain length of time each year. Obviously, it didn't make any difference who the resident was, because even though a cabin was built the first year, the Crooks didn't actually live there until 1932, and then only during July and August.

They moved from Windermere to establish an auto camp, complete with service station. If the station were still there, it would be almost on the highway directly in front of the present entrance gate. Across from the station, Crook and his son, Ray, built seven cabins in 1933–34, all fronting on the road. No sign of the station remains, and the only major evidence of development on the other side of the highway is the concrete floor of the washroom.

The washroom had separate facilities for men and women, including hot showers. Water was gravity-fed from a 3800 litre tank on a tower located next to the gas station, and heated by an oil burner. Cabins rented for $2 to $4 a night (one bed or two) and gas was advertised at $0.36 a gallon (nearly 10 cents a liter)—expensive for those days.

There were homesteads on both sides of the Crooks, another next to the Kootenay River picnic site, and a couple in the vicinity of Dolly Varden Creek. Ray Crook, who now lives in Invermere, said he couldn't understand why the government even offered homesteads in the Kootenay River valley. He claims it couldn't have been to encourage agriculture, because the growing season was so short. Crook remembers summers when potatoes froze in the ground.

The Crook family lived on the site from 1933 to 1956, when the government acquired the land. Charles Crook, who helped build the original highway, was killed while doing roadwork in 1945. His grave is located in the northwest corner of the meadows.

Park your car at the gate and pay homage to a Kootenay pioneer.

km 37.5 (57.0)

Above: In mid-summer, the meadows at Kootenay Crossing are transformed by countless yellow cinquefoil. Photo Bob Hahn.

Fireroad to Mount Daer Lookout: This lookout is located on the east side of the highway. As on all the fireroads, a locked gate prevents all but hikers and cyclists from going farther. This spur road crosses the Upper Kootenay River and links up with the East Kootenay fireroad. It's 13 km to the abandoned lookout, but you may have to ford the creek to get there. Most cyclists choose to travel along Hector Gorge, a distance of 9 km.

Speed Zone: Seasonal speed limits may be in place in this section of the park. These are not just for the benefit of people. This area is frequented by a variety of animals, but especially wolves travelling through the Kootenay River valley. Several of the canines have been killed on the highway here, including two in 1998. Slow down and keep your eyes open. Your chances of hitting a wolf are less and your chances of seeing one are better. It's one of those win-win situations.

km 42.5 (52.0)

Animals of virtually every species are killed on the park highway. Slow down for wildlife. Photo Bob Hahn.

Kootenay Crossing Exhibit: This display tells the story of early days when the mountain wilderness was primarily a playground for the wealthy. It details the history of the highway and describes the opening ceremony in 1923 (see page 16).

Off-highway cycling is only allowed on fireroads such as the West Kootenay one seen here. Photo Bob Hahn.

Cyclists in the park should be wary of drivers who treat the wide shoulders as an extra lane. Photo Bob Hahn.

Biking in Kootenay

The park highway is well designed for bicycle touring, with wide, paved shoulders, but beware of drivers who consider the shoulder an extra lane. Exercise special caution through Sinclair Canyon (especially in the Iron Gates Tunnel) where the road is narrower.

Many cyclists participate in a classic cycle tour called the Golden Triangle. The triangle between Castle Junction, Radium and Golden is 313 km long. Cyclists experience high mountain passes, and can explore waterfalls and canyons along the way. The entire trip is on paved roads and about two-thirds of the route has a wide shoulder giving good clearance from vehicles. The section from Radium Hot Springs to Golden has very narrow shoulders, however, the traffic on this section tends to be lighter. The trip winds through three national parks: Banff, Kootenay and Yoho, and usually takes about three days. Cyclists should be prepared for all weather conditions—it can snow any month of the year in Kootenay National Park.

It is best to stock up on supplies before entering the park, as the only place to pick up food and basic supplies in Kootenay is at Vermilion Crossing, 63 km from the West Entrance.

Mountain biking is allowed only on fireroads in the Kootenay River valley. These fireroads are also open for hiking and horse use. Please ride with care and give the right-of-way to hikers and horses. The main access points for the fireroads are Kootenay Crossing, McLeod Meadows and Crooks Meadows. More information and park trail maps are available at the information centres. There are many good mountain bike routes outside the park as well.

There is good mountain biking at the Nipika Touring Centre about 14 km south of Highway 93 off Settler's Road. A lodge and cabin offer service by prior arrangement.

Consult *Backcountry Biking in the Canadian Rockies* by Doug Eastcott for more information on mountain biking in the area.

km 42.9 (51.6) **Kootenay Crossing Warden Station:** If you have problems or questions about some unusual situation, someone might be in the office but there is no guarantee as the wardens are often out in the park. An outside radio-phone is provided for emergency use only.

Two mountain bike trails begin here: the north end of the Dolly Varden trail and the West Kootenay trail that extends to the park boundary (12.8 km).

km 43.3 (51.2) **Kootenay Crossing Bridge:** You'll probably notice that the Kootenay River flowing under this bridge looks quite different from the Kootenay River you've been following, if you are coming from the south. Other than at spring run-off, the upper Kootenay is a small, incredibly clear stream that comes from lakes outside the park.

But it becomes a different river after combining with the glacier-fed Vermilion near the Dolly Varden picnic area. Obviously, it's the Vermilion that is loaded with the rock flour (suspended particles of rock, ground from the mountains by glaciers) that gives the water such a beautiful, milky turquoise colour. The big mystery is why the name Kootenay has been retained, as it is obviously a tributary of the larger Vermilion.

km 44.1 (50.4) **Kootenay Pond:** Geologists classify this as a kettle pond. Kettles are formed by the melting of a block of glacial ice that had been covered by gravel and other material. The depression left by the melting ice has become filled with water.

There is neither an inlet nor an outlet to Kootenay Pond, but at one time this body of water was stocked with trout. The fish are now gone, leaving the pond as habitat for a variety of waterfowl and a breeding place for amphibians such as the western toad, the long-toed salamander and the wood frog.

Above the bridge, the Kootenay River is a small, clear stream. Photo Bob Hahn.

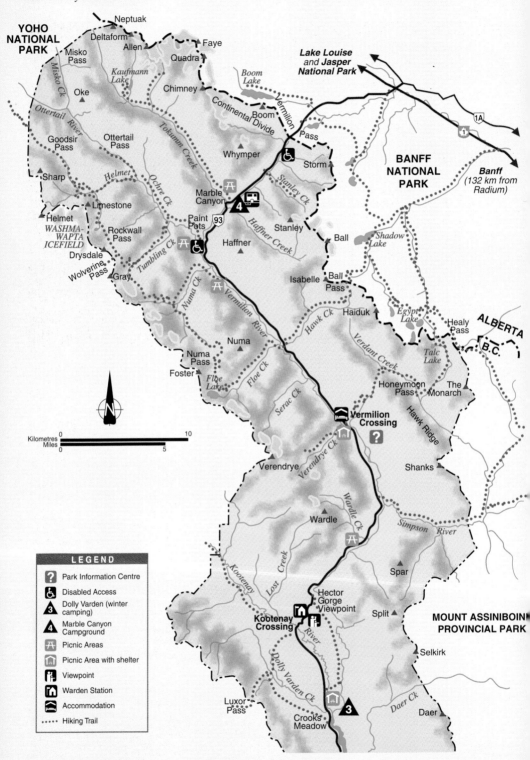

YOHO NATIONAL PARK

Neptuak

Deltaform
Allen

Faye

Misko Pass

Quadra

Kaufmann Lake

Misko Ck

Oke

Chimney

Boom Lake

Lake Louise and Jasper National Park

Continental Divide

Boom

Vermilion

Boom Pass

1A

1

Ottertail River

Goodsir Pass

Ottertail Pass

Tokumm Creek

Whymper

Storm

BANFF NATIONAL PARK

Banff (132 km from Radium)

Sharp

Helmet

Limestone

Marble Canyon

4

Stanley Ck

Stanley

Shadow Lake

HELMET WASHMA-WAPTA ICEFIELD

Rockwall Pass

Ochre Ck

Paint Pots

93

Haffner Creek

Ball

Drysdale

Gray

Tumbling Ck

Haffner

Wolverine Pass

Numa Ck

Vermilion River

Isabelle

Ball Pass

Hawk Ck

Haiduk

Egypt Lake

Healy Pass

ALBERTA B.C.

Numa

Verdant Creek

Talc Lake

Numa Pass

Foster

Floe Lake

Floe Ck

Serac Ck

Honeymoon Pass

The Monarch

Vermilion Crossing

?

Hawk Ridge

Verendrye

Verendrye Ck

Shanks

Wardle

Wardle Ck

Simpson River

Kootenay

Lost Creek

Spar

MOUNT ASSINIBOINE PROVINCIAL PARK

Hector Gorge Viewpoint

Split

Kootenay Crossing

Selkirk

River

Luxor Pass

Dolly Varden Ck

3

Daer Ck

Crooks Meadow

Daer

Kilometres 0 — 10
Miles 0 — 5

N

km 46.9 (47.6)

Mount Wardle has the greatest concentration of mountain goats in the park.

Hector Gorge Viewpoint: A small parking area on the east side of the highway gives visitors coming from the direction of Radium Hot Springs their first view of the Vermilion River. The gorge is a far cry from the Grand Canyon or other spectacular North American chasms, but it harbors some of the most exciting rapids in the Vermilion-Kootenay River system. At a distance they don't look all that forbidding—and they're not to experienced river rats—but extra caution is necessary for most boaters to negotiate them.

This is an excellent spot to take out binoculars and scan the mountain slopes across the highway to the north. That immense chunk of upthrust limestone is Mount Wardle, and it harbors the largest population of mountain goats (see page 117) in the park: about 75-100.

Spotting wildlife at long distances is a skill that has to be developed. I've often tried to help individuals see an animal that was very obvious to me, but they couldn't find anything. It's not enough just to know the colour of the animals—mountain goats are off-white—but you also need to have some idea of scale. When looking from the viewpoint, goats on Mount Wardle appear as little more than white dots, even through a 40-power spotting scope. If you locate something that looks promising, watch long enough to see if it moves. Of course, if the animals are lying down, the only movements are cud chewing or ear twitching and that's hard to detect on a dot, no matter how white it is.

As with most wildlife, goats are most active in the morning and evening when groups of two to five or more may be observed moving over the green subalpine slopes. You might also see some goats in the higher barren-looking rocks, but there isn't as much food up there. If you can't find any of the shaggy creatures, don't despair—just read the next entry.

Top—Mountain lady's slipper, mid-left— calypso orchids, mid- right—white bog orchid, bottom— yellow lady's slipper. Photos Bob Hahn.

Tropical Kootenay

So you had trouble choosing between a trip to the mountains or a visit to some tropical paradise full of exotic flowers. Kootenay just might fit the bill. There isn't an abundance of sandy beaches, and no palm trees, but exotic flowers— how about 22 species of orchids?

The time to enjoy the greatest variety of these delicate beauties is early summer. Lovely pink calypso

*Handbook of the Canadian Rockies

orchids, aka fairy-slippers, dress up many of the trails in the park. Take the time to search out the tiny round-leaved orchid, "…angels in purple-dotted white robes, with mauve hats and wings…."* Look for showy mountain lady's slippers with their white globes and three long brownish-purple sepals sticking out like overstarched shirt collars. A similar species, the yellow lady's slipper, is also rare in the park, but can be abundant in some of the surrounding mountain areas.

White bog orchids, with their spikes of white flowers, are common in damp meadows. Don't get them confused with ladies'-tresses, where the flowers spiral around the stem, and the scent is vanilla (vanilla flavouring actually comes from the fruit of a tropical orchid).

Most orchids have a lovely scent, which is their come-on to insect pollinators—that even includes mosquitoes. The unique design of the flowers is also important for successful pollination. The peculiar structure ensures that each visiting insect picks up pollen on the same body part. Otherwise, the next flower the bug visits may not be fertilized.

Unfortunately, we humans like to collect beautiful things, and in doing so we often destroy them. That is the case with orchids. No matter how carefully you gather these delicate plants to transplant in your garden, they usually die. What you can't gather is the complicated system of microorganisms in the soil that is the orchid's life-support system. Of course, if you're caught with pilfered orchids in the park, you may never see your family again! But that shouldn't be your main deterrent. Leave the flowers be, so other folks have the opportunity to savour their beauty—just like you do.

km 47.8 (46.7)

Goat Lick: Drive carefully down and around the corner from the viewpoint and start scanning the base of the light-coloured cliffs next to the highway. You might be lucky enough to find that some of those "white spots" have taken on substance, and are, in fact, right beside the road. The cliffs contain a variety of minerals necessary for the well being of mountain goats. As the early summer plant growth higher on the mountain doesn't contain enough calcium and copper, a trip down to the lick is the "in" thing for nannies. They especially need the minerals for new hair growth and lactation. Of course, the kids come along.

Nanny goats frequently bring their kids down to mineral licks near the highway in early summer. Photo Bob Hahn.

Slow down and be careful, but don't stop until you can get completely off the road. The biggest danger here comes from the human animals who wouldn't slow down if their mothers were on the road, let alone a bunch of goat-watching strangers.

Stop only briefly and stay in your vehicle. It is important not to disturb the goats. As with most other wild park residents, they may seem to ignore your presence. But if you come too close they get nervous. Animals can easily become stressed—just as you and I can. However, the goats can't hop in a car and travel a few thousand miles to escape that hemmed-in feeling. If you've come here to get some breathing room, give the animals the same break.

These goats may appear nonplussed, but it is much less stressful to the animals if visitors remain in their vehicles. Photo Bob Hahn.

A smoldering forest looks devastated, but new life springs from the ashes.

Forest Fires in our National Parks —Is Smokey Dead?

To keep our parks in as natural a state as possible we must ensure that all the natural processes that have shaped these scenic areas continue to do so. One of the most controversial of natural disturbances is fire. For nearly a century most park managers—as well as the general public—viewed forest fires as destructive processes to be extinguished as soon as possible. In fact, the main reason for founding the warden service in 1909 was to contend with forest fires.

Smokey the Bear, who came along in the 1950s, also emphasized the devastation of forest fires. He even put the entire blame on us with his classic line: "Only you can prevent forest fires." But fire, like the wind or rain, is a natural part of the ecosystem. Our success at suppressing forest fires is actually a threat to the ecosystem.

Instead of being the destructive force of Smokey's world, forest fires

benefit the ecosystem. They speed up the recycling of nutrients stored in wood, thus promoting new growth. In many parts of the world, especially tropical regions, the inhabitants depend on burn and slash farming because most of the available nutrients are bound up in vegetation. They may not understand the burning process—they just know it works. Even back in ancient Rome, the poet, Vergil, speculated about fire: "Often likewise it is well to burn barren fields and consume the light stubble in crackling flame: whether that earth thence conceives secret strength and sustenance, or all her evil is melted away and her useless moisture sweats out in the fire...."

Not only does fire make the more heat-resistant nutrients readily available in the ashes, but the shady forest canopy is now gone and sun-loving plants flourish. The new growth attracts deer, elk and a

Continued on page 72

km 48.8 (45.7)   **Wardle Creek Picnic Area:** This a cozy spot close to the small creek. Watch for the sign and turn just north of the bridge. You'll have lots of company here—in the form of Columbian ground squirrels. Enjoy the little creatures, but keep your distance—they have fleas.

Take a short walk upstream and you'll find a set of heavy metal wheels, complete with axle, imbedded in the sand. They may have come from some of the road-building equipment used in the 1920s.

km 55.5 (39.0)   **Animal Lick:** This is the only marked lick in the park, but that doesn't mean you should stop and hold your breath until an animal appears. For example, I once did an evening program where I showed a picture of a moose in the lick. Afterwards, a woman came up and said, "I'm glad you showed that picture, because we've been driving from Alberta to Kootenay for 30 years, and I've never seen anything at that lick!"

The lick itself is really that little puddle of murky water, and the animals, usually moose, slurp up the horrid looking stuff, rather than actually licking something. I don't know if the water has ever been analyzed to determine its contents, but it's probably rich in sulphur. Moose need sulphur for healthy hair just like mountain goats do.

km 56.7 (37.8)   **Simpson Monument:** George Simpson's hurried trip through the Rockies in 1841 is immortalized here (see page 12). Situated almost due east is the Simpson River valley, the route of his expedition. Simpson was in such a hurry, he probably didn't even take the time to look back and enjoy the view.

Looking to the south, you may be able to see evidence of a fire that burned on the west slope of Spar Mountain in 1991. A few days after it was discovered, there were five helicopters using the flats between the monument and the Vermilion River as a landing area. Extra aircraft appeared because the fire bordered Mount Assiniboine Provincial Park. Thus, B.C. Parks personnel had to be called upon for consultation. After an aerial survey, their recommendations were characteristic of the new philosophy relating to forest fires. They elected to suppress this fire only where it posed a danger to facilities, like the Surprise Creek Cabin.

Moose slurp the water to obtain sulphates and other minerals. Photo Bob Hahn.

Kootenay officials agreed, and, as much as possible, the fire was allowed to run its course. Carefully watched by the park's fire crew, it smoldered on and off for a couple of months—and was reported a few hundred times by diligent visitors.

*Dropping fire
retardent is
expensive and it
may also be
counterproduc-
tive in terms of
park mandates.*

whole new population of mammals and birds. Instead of destroying most life—large mammals are rarely trapped by a fire and the majority of smaller creatures probably escape also—the resulting variety of habitats created by a fire actually promotes biodiversity.

Bringing fire back into the ecosystem is not easy. Wildfires cannot be permitted to burn freely in our parks, because there is too much risk to people and property. Yet parks are now mandated to maintain ecological integrity, which means having complete, healthy, functioning ecosystems. This is impossible unless all natural processes (like fire) are allowed to occur.

Suppression of wildfires will always be necessary in our parks, but fire management must be more than that. Fire must be used as a tool to help restore natural ecosystems. Prescribed burns have become an important part of the fire management plan in Kootenay and most other Canadian national parks. Most of the prescribed burns are done in the spring and early summer. In remote areas, under certain conditions, fires started by lightning are also treated as pre-

*A firefighter
is lowered to
do his job.*

scribed fires and allowed to burn (see Simpson Monument on the preceding page).

To date, the prescribed burns in Kootenay have been small. Fire managers must be very cautious in this long, narrow park where boundaries are always nearby. But with each burn the knowledge of fire behaviour increases. Coupled with scientific studies, this new information will help Parks Canada to modify the prescribed fire program—and enhance the ecological integrity of our national treasures.

*Most forest fires in
Kootenay are
caused by lightning.*

This fire provided a training ground not only for local crews, but also for crews from other jurisdictions. Two years later, their experience paid off. In the hot, dry summer of 1994 fires blazed throughout the entire western half of North America. Again, crews were called in to contain a large blaze west of the Simpson Monument on Mount Shanks. At times the flames flared 50 or more metres into the sky, and the fire stretched to treeline. Fire headquarters sprang up near the parking area, which became off-limits to all but firefighters. With other fires in the vicinity, the area around the monument buzzed with activity. The arid conditions made it essential to bring these fires under control. Yet, despite all the effort, pillars of smoke occasionally drifted skyward even after the rains of autumn came. Mother Nature always likes to have the last word.

km 57.4 (37.1) **Simpson River Trailhead:** A parking area and bridge mark the beginning of this easy trail to Mount Assiniboine Provincial Park. Turn right at the locked gate on the fireroad. It's only 8 km to the park boundary, but to reach Mount Assiniboine (named after the Stoney tribe), plan on a good two-day hike.

In late summer it was common to see stock trucks and horse trailers parked here. They belonged to outfitters and other hunters who had ridden into the provincial park where hunting is legal. However, since the mid-'90s, firearms and game must travel by a different route—usually Settler's Road and then up Cross River.

As indicated by its name, the trail follows the sparkling Simpson River. Why it's called a river instead of a creek is a mystery to me, because it's not very big.

The Simpson River is a lovely small stream that harbors some nice cutthroat trout. Don't make the mistake I did on a September fishing trip and fight through the brush to reach the water. Just stay on the trail and be patient. You'll soon be streamside. By the way, I did

Mount Assiniboine is one of the highest and most spectacular Matterhorn-type peaks in the Canadian Rockies. Courtesy Kootenay National Park. Photo Hans Fuhrer.

Mount Assiniboine Provincial Park

The Alpine Club of Canada can take credit for encouraging the B.C. government to protect this beautiful area in the early part of the century. Their efforts were rewarded in 1922, when a little over 5000 ha was set aside as Mount Assiniboine Provincial Park. At one time there was talk of this small triangle, sandwiched between Banff and Kootenay national parks, being absorbed by its neighbours. But the park never changed hands, and 51 years after its origin the size was increased seven-fold to 38,600 ha.

This is truly a high-altitude park. The entire area lies above 1500 m. While stunning mountain peaks are the main attraction, there is also an abundance of lovely alpine lakes. Some of them have achieved a reputation for excellent cutthroat trout fishing, but, as in virtually all high lakes, success is unpredictable.

One thing that *is* predictable is the beauty of meadows ablaze with colourful wildflowers in mid-summer. You may also see elk and mule deer grazing amidst the blooms, while chirping Columbian ground squirrels object to their presence. High on the peaks, mountain goats may leisurely view the activity below as golden-mantled ground squirrels scurry by.

This is a hiker's park, although horseback trips are not uncommon. Also, helicopters bring guests to Mount Assiniboine Lodge. A limited number of beds can be rented in four cabins located near the lake, but it's first come, first served during the summer (reservations are required from December 1 to May 31). The main camping area is on the west side of Lake Magog (for a fee). Other campgrounds and cabin shelters are scattered throughout the park, and these are often less crowded.

catch a few nice trout that clear autumn day, but the trip is memorable more for my face-to-face encounter with a curious and very large mountain lion than for any fish.

km 61.0 (33.5)   **View of Mount Assiniboine:** Watch for a small pull-off on the river side of the highway about 4 km past Simpson Monument (2.5 km south of Vermilion Crossing). If it's a clear day, look to the southwest for the tip of a pyramid-shaped mountain. This stretch of the highway is the only place in the park where you can see Mount Assiniboine, the Matterhorn of the Rockies, without climbing. The striking peak is the sixth highest mountain in the Canadian Rockies. Like all Matterhorn-type peaks, it was created when at least three cirque or hanging glaciers ground away from different sides.

km 63.2 (31.3)   **Vermilion River Crossing:** The Crossing is the only oasis between the hot springs and Alberta where you can load up on snacks, get a good meal or rent a bed. Visit the Information Centre to see some interesting displays and learn more about the park. If you are coming from the east this is the first place in Kootenay to get some specific answers to questions about the area. However, park staff at the Lake Louise or Banff information centres can supply you with basic maps and some information.

The Vermilion River, shown here, has a much larger drainage than the upper Kootenay River. Photo Bob Hahn.

The masked wood frog is at home in a cold environment.

The Icy Bandit

Can you imagine walking across the northern tundra above the Arctic Circle and seeing a masked frog? Well, believe it or not, it could happen. Seeing a frog that far north might be a shock to some people. These unique little (30–60 mm) cold-tolerant creatures are wood frogs, and they seem to roam almost anywhere their small legs take them.

Wood frogs are found all across Canada, often far from water, and at elevations up to 2500 m. In the spring, they swarm to the nearest pond for breeding and announce their presence in a most unmel-

odious way. It sounds like a flock of hoarse ducks. Not only can predators easily locate them from the racket, but the frogs don't make any attempt to remain inconspicuous. Several males may battle over a single female, until all but one drops off owing to fatigue.

The most incredible fact about wood frogs is their amazing ability to survive freezing winter temperatures with very little cover. They may simply crawl under a pile of leaves in the autumn, go to sleep and actually **freeze solid**! Yet, when placed in warm surroundings, these four-legged "ice cubes" will soon thaw and hop away.

In his naturalist's bible, *Handbook of the Canadian Rockies*, Ben Gadd reports that researchers have found that when the wood frog begins to freeze, its liver pumps out extraordinary amounts of glucose. The glucose, which is a type of sugar, sucks up moisture that would otherwise be lost from the cells during freezing. This prevents the dehydration that actually causes death by freezing. Even so, 50 per cent of the fluid in a hibernating wood frog is ice. Some cool customer, eh? And sweet, too.

Fishing in Kootenay National Park

Few people come to Kootenay National Park just for the fishing. There aren't many lakes and most of the streams are coloured by glacial silt. The icy water is too cold to support high populations of fish fodder such as insects and other invertebrates. Thus, don't expect to find as many fish as you would in nutrient-rich warmer waters. However, for the patient angler willing to wander a little farther from the highway, it is possible to find some decent fishing.

Regulations are always subject to change. You should pick up a copy of the current regulations at an Information Centre—a copy should come with your licence.

Anyone 16 or older must obtain a national park fishing permit. Provincial licences and regulations are not valid in Kootenay. No bait fishing is allowed. The daily limit of trout and char combined is two fish. Possession limits are the same. All bull trout must be released. Catch and release is encouraged for all species.

The first waters open to fishing are usually Cobb and Olive lakes, about mid-May. By July 1 all waters should be open, but check the current regulations.

Located across the highway, south of the bridge, is a picnic area complete with shelter and wood stove. A short trail also leads to the lower slopes of Mount Verendrye (3086 m).

The 4 km-long trail is good up to the crossing of Verendrye Creek—wear old shoes, because there is no bridge—and then it deteriorates. Trail maintenance is minimal or nonexistent because the section of the park between Mount Verendrye and Wardle is designated a primitive area—no trails or other development—owing to the large population of mountain goats. Actually, the best view of Verendrye's Matterhorn-like heights is from the highway north of the bridge.

Mount Verendrye marks the southern terminus of the Rockwall, a formidable 53 km-long limestone escarpment that forms the northwest boundary of the park (see map page 66).

km 63.6 (30.9) **Verdant Creek Trailhead:** Watch for an unpaved turn-off shortly above the northwest side of the bridge. This trail climbs steeply for 4.8 km to Honeymoon Pass (1970 m) and down the other side to Verdant Creek Campground (8.1 km). It's another 3.5 km to the warden cabin. Continue for 7.4 km to a small meadow. Look for a junction sign. Follow the left fork 2.3 km to Talc (Natalco) Lake, where remnants of an old mine are visible. If the wind is blowing, you may see the waterfall on the far side of this lonely lake change directions. Note: this trail has unbridged creek crossings. Caution is advised.

Hikers take a well-deserved break on the shores of beautiful Floe Lake. Photo Bob Hahn.

Hikers from Talc Lake look into Banff National Park. Photo Bob Hahn.

Talc Lake is rarely visited, but the right fork leads to one of the busiest backcountry areas in Banff, near Egypt Lake. A short distance east of Talc is the point where the two national parks and Mount Assiniboine Provincial Park come together.

km 71.7 (22.8)   **Floe Lake Trailhead:** (10.2 km one way, elevation gain 732 m) Floe Lake, so named for the miniature icebergs that often float in this turquoise gem, nestles at the base of a sheer 1000 m-high cliff. Directly above the lake a small glacier, the source of the ice floes, clings precariously to the sheer limestone wall. No wonder this is one of the most popular backcountry destinations in the park. Backpackers doing the entire length of the Rockwall from south to north spend their first night in the campsite here.

Floe is also a rewarding but challenging day hike (warm-up on some of the shorter trails first). After crossing the Vermilion River, which is coloured by glacial sediment, the trail follows a very gentle grade for the first 4 km. Avalanche slopes provide the only openings in the forest cover and offer good grazing for elk, deer, moose and bears. Keep your eyes open.

At approximately 8 km a series of steep switchbacks up the headwall tests the best of hikers. Just when you wonder if the world will ever be level again, the trail tops the ridge and you know the grunts have all been worthwhile. This is never more true than when the alpine flowers are in full glory, and again, in the fall, when the subalpine (Lyall's) larches turn the mountain slopes to gold.

Horses in Kootenay

If you encounter any parties on horseback in the park, they will most likely consist of either wardens or members of the trail crew. Horseback trips for private individuals are permitted on most of the longer park trails, but these are rare. After all, there are only two designated campsites where horse parties can camp overnight: Verdant Creek and Helmet Falls. Use of facilities at a warden patrol cabin is strictly forbidden.

For backcountry horse travel requiring an overnight stay, a park grazing permit is required. There is a nominal fee for the permits that may be obtained up to 90 days prior to departure. A wilderness pass is also required.

Pre-trip planning should include:
– Date of arrival and departure
– Where you wish to go and when
– Number of both horses and people

Group size is not to exceed 10 people. Maximum stay at any grazing area is three nights. In addition to natural graze, rely on alfalfa cubes and prepared grains rather than hay or alfalfa. Otherwise, non-native plants may be introduced.

Horses should be hobbled rather than being picketed or tied up overnight, to minimize ground damage. They should not be brought within 50 m of a campsite unless you are packing or unpacking.

Don't tie stock to trees or bushes. A good alternative is to stretch a rope between two trees and use it as a temporary hitching rail.

Make sure to scatter all manure when you are finished. This is a good policy whenever the horses have had their movements restricted for some time.

There are no stables in the park, but horses can be rented at a variety of places in the Columbia Valley.

Packtrains like this are rare in the park. Horses are usually hauling supplies for the wardens or trail crew. Photo Danny Catt.

km 71.7 (22.8)

The hanging glacier on Mount Ball is a stunning climax for hikers who venture out on the Hawk Creek trail. Photo Bob Hahn.

Hawk Creek Trailhead: (9.7 km one way, elevation gain 844 m) Access is across the highway from the Floe Lake parking area. In sharp contrast to the popular Floe Lake route, hikers rarely meet anyone else on this trail. It might stem from the fact that the author of one popular hiking guide questions the intelligence of anyone who would willingly choose to hike this trail. Well, if you want an easy hike with beautiful vistas, colourful alpine flowers and the solitude mentioned above, this trail is a great choice.

The path initially passes through subalpine forest with the sounds of cascading Hawk Creek in the distance. It's possible to find a half-dozen different species of orchids in the shade.

Eventually, the trail breaks out into talus slopes with excellent views of the Rockwall across the valley. Hawk Creek is now visible. Watch for waterfalls. A few minor switchbacks are briefly encountered at about km 7 as the trail swings north to Ball Pass (2182 m). This is about the only break in an otherwise gradual trek.

The last kilometre of the trail leads through open stands of subalpine larch and a magnificent display of wildflowers. From the pass there are stunning views of the hanging glacier on Mount Ball as well as a look at Shadow Lake in Banff National Park. Your only company may be a resident white-tailed ptarmigan.

km 80.0 (14.5)

Numa Creek Picnic Area: The highlight of a stop here is Numa Falls, only a short walk from the parking area. The water doesn't drop very far, but the glistening, sculptured rocks attest to its persistent force—an obstinacy far beyond human potential. The view from the rustic bridge is the best, both of the falls and Vermilion Canyon below. Walls of the small canyon are striated limestone slabs with hardy plants springing from every available niche.

The American dipper exercises on streamside rocks before walking underwater to find supper. Photo Bob Hahn.

Feathered Aerobics

Aerobics are everywhere: on TV, at the video store, on the bookshelves, in the gyms. Yet the last place you would expect to see a demonstration of this craze for exercise is alongside a cold mountain stream in the Canadian Rockies. However, watch closely and sooner or later you'll see a stubby gray bird perched on a creekside rock doing knee bends. That's where its name—dipper—comes from. It's also called water ouzel, but that's a mistake. Although similar-looking, the water ouzel of Europe is a different species.

Dippers are unique little birds. They are usually all by their lonesome, doing their own thing. One of their "things" is walking on the stream bottom, picking off unsuspecting insects and other small invertebrates. A dipper's toes are well adapted to grip rocks in the streambed, making this possible. However, they actually spend more time "flying" submerged than they do walking. The short, stiff wings seem better designed for underwater manoeuvres than for aerial acrobatics. But the dipper flies quite

well when it has to—as when migrating to reach a watershed with enough open water in the dead of winter. Other special adaptations for diving include movable flaps to close the nostrils and transparent membranes for eye protection. The plumage is extra thick, and virtually impervious to cold air and water. The preen gland, which secretes waterproofing oil, is 10 times larger than that of other songbirds.

Dippers are about the size of robins, but with their short, upturned tail and compact body they look like oversize wrens. Males and females are both the same slate-gray colour, but they do have white eyelids.

Nests are built under an overhang near running water—often under a waterfall. The structures are dome-shaped balls of moss, with an entrance hole facing down toward the water. The abundant moisture keeps the moss green, disguising the nest. About three weeks after hatching, the young dive into the stream. They learn to swim before they learn to fly.

The dipper's beautiful song is often masked by the chatter of the fast-moving stream, but there is no mistaking it during the dead of winter when snow and ice have muted most other sounds. The melody is startling in the silence, and even more so is the sight of the little bird, diving into a frigid pool when the air temperature is well below freezing.

If you miss your daily aerobics while on vacation, take a hike along one of Kootenay's tumbling creeks and watch for a dark-coloured bird zooming upstream no more than a metre above the surface. The American dipper won't go far, and when it stops, feel free to join in on the knee bends. Better leave the underwater walks to the bird, though.

The glistening, sculpted rocks at Numa Falls attest to its persistent force. Photo Bob Hahn.

Numa Creek Trail: (6.4 km one way, elevation gain 145 m) The trail beyond the bridge climbs gradually through a lush forest of subalpine fir and Engelmann spruce to a major junction with the Rockwall trail. Before deciding to travel any farther, make sure you've faithfully completed some gentle acclimating hikes, because it's a long, hard grunt to the top in either direction from here.

Numa Creek Campground (1525 m) is less than half a kilometre to the left. Continue on beyond the campground 6.8 km to Numa Pass (2355 m), the highest point on the Rockwall trail. Spectacular views help to compensate hikers for the steep climb. Beautiful Floe Lake is another 2.7 km beyond the pass, but the route is mainly downhill through meadows of alpine flowers, especially in late summer.

To the right from the junction is Tumbling Pass (2273 m), a distance of 5.3 km. This avalanche-prone route provides good foraging for grizzly bears, so take precautions. Views of Tumbling Glacier reward the persistent hiker. Descend from the pass to Tumbling Creek Campground (2.5 km).

Snow often makes it difficult to access this high country until mid-July or later. The information centres can supply up-to-date reports on trail conditions.

km 84.7 (9.8)   **The Paint Pots:** Before you reach the Paint Pots parking area coming from the south, notice the rusty looking banks along the west side of the Vermilion River. You'll see a great deal more of this reddish-orange, iron-rich clay or ochre by walking the hard-surfaced 1.5 km trail to the three cold springs designated as the Paint Pots. The trail is self guiding with interpretive signs that describe the history and significance of the area to aboriginal groups. It is wheelchair accessible as far as the suspension bridge over the Vermilion River. Just beyond the bridge, a trail to the right leads 2.7 km to Marble Canyon.

In early summer, the riverbanks and even the ochre flats are graced by a variety of wildflowers. Especially striking are the pink bird's-eye primroses found in the damp sections of ochre alongside the trail. Watch for tiny violet-like flowers on a single stem, jutting from basal, elongated pale green leaves with curled edges. These plants are butterworts, and they are meat eaters! Tiny insects become attached to the sticky leaves and are digested by the plant's own juices.

Avalanches are another way nature opens up the forest to promote biodiversity. Courtesy Kootenay National Park. Photo Hans Fuhrer.

Danger—Avalanche

It is not uncommon when driving through any mountainous area to see a sign warning: DANGER—AVALANCHE AREA. NO STOPPING. As you drive through such an area in the whiteness of winter, it's hard not to imagine a huge wall of snow careening down the mountain, smashing trees and anything else in its path. While your imagination runs wild, perhaps you unconsciously pick up speed and get a crick in your neck from straining to see uphill without taking your eyes from the road. The last thing you want to do is honk the horn, for you've heard how the smallest noise can trigger a massive slide.

Actually, it takes a lot more noise than that to start an avalanche. In Kootenay, avalanches rarely pose any problem for drivers thanks to an active avalanche control program. Yet, avalanche slopes are much in evidence throughout the park, especially in the north end. They can be readily identified, even from far away, as narrow bands of light green foliage,

aligned vertically, just like ski runs. Once these paths are established, it's certain snow slides will occur there again, but not necessarily every year. Conditions have to be just right. A combination of snow depth, temperature, steepness, wind direction and wind velocity all come into play.

While avalanches are an obvious danger to any living thing in their path, they are also extremely beneficial. Just like forest fires, avalanches aid biodiversity by opening up the forest. The new vegetation that springs up in a slide path—the shrubs, especially willows, plus wildflowers and grasses—provide essential food for large mammals such as moose, elk and grizzly bears. Smaller mammals and a variety of birds also frequent avalanche slopes.

Take the time to stop off the highway and scan a few slide paths, especially in early summer. You might be rewarded by the sight of a moose browsing in the willows, or even of an elusive grizzly bear digging the bulbs of glacier lilies. Happy viewing!

Evidence of man's most recent mining activities can be seen in the ochre flats. Some of the old machinery was probably used for a few years after Kootenay became a park in 1920. Of course, the aboriginal peoples visited the area long before anyone else even knew about the area. The Ktunaxa believed that a great thunder spirit resided in the springs and spoke to them in a flute-like voice. They also thought that the dried ochre, mixed with fish oil or melted animal fat, gave them special powers when painted on their bodies before going into battle. The vermilion was also traded to other tribes.

km 84.7 (9.8)   **Ochre Creek Trailhead:** Park your car in the Paint Pots parking area and follow the crowds up the nature trail to experience some of the best wilderness hiking in the park. When you reach the springs, where most folks are reversing directions, your journey could be just beginning. Another 4.4 km up the trail is a junction. Turn left to follow Tumbling Creek. If you continue right from the junction, along Ochre Creek for another 2.3 km, the trail again forks: left to Helmet Falls (8.6 km) and right to Ottertail Pass (3.3 km) and Yoho National Park. There is another trail to Yoho over Goodsir Pass (7.6 km to the park boundary) that starts just before Helmet Falls Campground. Before considering any journey into

Ochre from the sacred Paint Pots was very important to the aboriginal peoples. Photo Bob Hahn.

Yoho, check for trail closures. There are restrictions in place to protect grizzly bear habitat and reduce the chance of bear/human encounters.

    The extensive system of trails and campgrounds beyond the Paint Pots makes it possible to do a spectacular circuit, retracing only the initial 4.4

Helmet Falls could arguably be the second highest falls in Canada, but beauty isn't measured in statistics. Photo Gillean Daffern.

Hikers come from all over the world to experience the grandeur of the Rockwall. Photo Gillean Daffern.

Golden subalpine larches near Wolverine Pass make for a memorable late September day. Photo Bob Hahn.

km (the complete circuit is 38.2 km). You need a minimum of three days, but take more if you can. Plan to spend the first night at Tumbling Creek Campground (11 km). Allow yourself enough time on your hike in to enjoy and photograph the numerous waterfalls on Tumbling Creek. If you have the time, stay at the campground at least two nights and do some exploring. You can build up your stamina by either heading south to Tumbling Pass (2.5 km) or taking the easier climb to Wolverine Pass (3.3 km) in the other direction. It's easy to lose yourself in the alpine splendour near Wolverine, the only significant gap in the 53 km length of the Rockwall.

Of course, if you explore the country around Wolverine, you'll be re-tracing some steps when you make the trek to Helmet Falls Campground (11.9 km). But you could tread the same mountain paths every day for a year and see something different every time. It might be anything from an unknown delicate mountain bloom to a pair of husky velvet-antlered mule deer bucks. What's more likely is simply the vagaries of light on the heights of Mount Drysdale or even a light dusting of snow, no matter what the season.

John Pitcher and the author ham it up for a Kootenay Gothic. Photo Bob Hahn.

Watch for mountain goats as you traverse Limestone Pass and start the steep descent to Helmet Falls Campground. The furry alpine climbers are also common on the sheer cliffs near Helmet Falls. Some of the best views of the impressive 350 m-high falls are from this section of the trail.

You won't want to leave the high country, no matter when you come.

Early morning mist rises from frigid Tokumm Creek and the cold confines of Marble Canyon. Photo Bob Hahn.

Of course, the incredible geological features, especially the Rockwall, are always the main attractions, but these are seasonally enhanced. In summer the kaleidoscope of colours in the meadow flower "gardens" can be overwhelming, and, come fall, slopes blaze with the orange and gold of Lyall's larches. This is what national parks are all about, in living colour.

km 87.0 (7.5) **Fire Crew Headquarters:** The buildings on the south side of the highway next to the bridge over Haffner Creek are used by the First Attack Fire Crew in the summer. They do not have a telephone (the nearest phone is 12 km north at Storm Mountain Lodge) and there is no reason to stop unless you want to report a fire.

km 87.3 (7.2) **Marble Canyon:** To those who say the hot springs are the main attraction in Kootenay National Park, Marble Canyon fans would shout, "You're all wet!" Marble's beauty can be appreciated again and again and many repeat visitors testify to this fact.

The trail is less than a kilometre long, but some climbing is involved. Interpretive signs explain the never-ending processes at work in the canyon, but no signs can express the feeling of wonder experienced by viewers.

Notice the temperature change as you stand on the first bridge. A combination of cold water and the inability of sunlight to penetrate the depths frequently limits the temperature in the canyon to only half as much as the surrounding area. This has a pronounced effect on vegetation (see page 90).

The trail to the left just beyond the first bridge leads back to a footbridge over the Vermilion River located a short distance below the parking lot. It's a nice little jaunt to take on your return and offers close-up views of some interesting potholes. It's also possible to continue on downstream 2.7 km to the Paint Pots trail.

As you climb higher, crossing and recrossing the canyon on a series of seven rustic wooden bridges, Tokumm Creek seems to be going in the opposite direction. Maximum depth of the canyon is usually recorded as 40 m, but some estimates go as high as 60 m (I'm inclined to agree with the latter). At times, the icy turquoise waters of Tokumm Creek are hidden by the walls of this narrow chasm. A natural bedrock bridge actually spans the gap at one point. **WARNING:** Do not try to walk across. People have fallen to their deaths in this canyon.

Marble Canyon seems to increase in depth the higher you go. Photo Bob Hahn.

Marble Canyon is the result of two natural forces: mountain building and erosion. Most obvious is the grinding and scouring action of rushing Tokumm Creek, especially below the waterfall. Look for potholes, formed when rocks were swirled incessantly by the turbulent waters.

*Purple saxifrage.
Photo Gillean
Daffern.*

Misplaced Plants

Purple saxifrage is a lovely flowering plant, well worth a few pictures. Getting the photos is going to take a little effort, though. Probably the easiest way is to slip on your hiking boots and head for alpine country (above 2000 m), because purple saxifrage flourishes in cooler areas. It even grows as far north as Ellesmere Island in the Arctic. Make your trip early in the summer, because purple saxifrage blooms just as the snow goes.

However, there is an alternative to the long climb. Just hike the short trail along Marble Canyon and look down. In a few places you might see a low-growing plant sporting numerous bell-shaped, violet blossoms. You are looking at purple saxifrage far from its normal alpine environment. The problem is that it will probably be clinging precariously to the sheer canyon wall. That limits picture-taking only to photographers with big telephoto lenses.

So maybe you won't get your picture to show the folks back home. They won't miss it. But what you *can* do is amaze them with the fact that not only purple saxifrage, but at least 20 other alpine plants grow in the unusual microclimate of Marble Canyon. Even in the canyon, you will find a difference in distribution. For instance, plants that thrive in the most humid environment are likely to be found closer to the waterfall.

Microclimates are part of any environment. They are simply small areas with some climatic factor(s) that make them different from their surroundings. The area may be shadier, rockier, drier, windier or different in a combination of ways. The differences affect plant growth and the animal life that depends on it. You might note the same thing at home, just by comparing the north side of your home to the south side.

Marble Canyon's differences are most noticeable on a warm summer day. Researchers have recorded August temperatures in the canyon 8-10 degrees cooler than in the surrounding forest. You'll feel the difference as soon as you reach the first bridge. So keep your eyes open. You may find the unexpected. Don't get your hopes too high, though—polar bears are yet to be seen this far south.

*Top: Mountain avens.
Bottom: White heather.
Photos Gillean Daffern.*

Tokumm Creek flows through Prospector's Valley, named for the explorers who found small deposits of lead and zinc there. Photo Bob Hahn.

Less obvious is the minor fault along which the canyon has been cut. Faults are weak zones, easily eroded by running water, and Tokumm Creek has done its work along this one. The rock on either side of the fault is dolomite (magnesium carbonate), not marble. Marble is limestone (calcium carbonate) that has recrystallized under heat and pressure. Nevertheless, debris in the swirling waters of the canyon has polished some of the dolomite to a sheen characteristic of the finest marble. No wonder someone made a mistake in naming this chasm.

Watch for small grey birds flying above the rushing waters, or bobbing up and down on a streamside rock. The latter habit has given these interesting creatures the name "dipper" (see page 82). Most prominent at the start of the trail are the plump, striped golden-mantled ground squirrels. They are larger than chipmunks, don't hoist their tails vertically like their smaller cousins, and have stripes only on their backs, not on their cheeks.

A small picnic area with shelter is located above the toilets at the northeast end of the parking lot.

km 87.3 (7.2)   **Tokumm Creek Trailhead:** Located just to the right, as you start up the Marble Canyon trail, is another trail that leads to Kaufmann Lake (14.5 km) and the Fay Hut (13.6 km). Although this trail through Prospector's Valley leads toward Kootenay's highest mountain, Deltaform (3424 m), and some other spectacular alpine country—the backside of Banff's Valley of the Ten Peaks—it is usually snowfree before most of the other trails in the area. This apparent anomaly is a result of little change in elevation for the first 11 km to Fay Creek.

After crossing the creek, it's a different story, no matter which fork in the trail you choose. To the right is the steep climb to Fay Hut, administered by the Alpine Club of Canada. The left branch, to Kaufmann Lake, remains more gradual with a bit of climbing just below the lake.

Prospector's Valley was the scene of some early mining activity, with a small amount of lead and zinc removed. The remains of a few old mining buildings can still be found on the west side of the creek, not far above the upper end of Marble Canyon. Also quite evident in the same area is a multitude of moose and elk tracks. Avalanche slopes all along the valley are covered by the type of herbaceous shrubby growth that these ungulates love.

Fay Hut, built in 1927, was the first constructed by the Alpine Club of Canada.

High Luxury

Those who have stayed in the Fay Hut might not describe it as luxurious, but any roof over my head during inclement weather has always seemed like paradise. The hut is reached by following the Tokumm Creek trail for 13.6 km, starting at Marble Canyon. Mountaineers also occasionally come over from Moraine Lake in Banff using Wenkchemna Pass.

The hut, built in 1927, was the very first constructed by the Alpine Club of Canada. It is named for Charles E. Fay, an American climber who visited the Canadian Rockies and the Selkirk Mountains at least 25 times between 1890 and his death in 1930.

As you can imagine, years of fierce weather have taken their toll on the building. A windstorm in the 1960s brought down trees, severely damaging the roof. Visits decreased, and the hut was turned over to the park for maintenance. It was eventually closed in 1984.

Fortunately, a renovated Fay Hut reopened in 1991, again under the administration of the Alpine Club. Reservations for use of the hut are necessary. Contact the A.C.C. in Canmore, Alberta, at 403-678-3200.

Camping at Marble

As you might expect, this campground has the highest elevation of the three drive-in campgrounds. Like McLeod, self-registration is required for the 66 unserviced (no hookups) sites, with all pertinent information being found in the little kiosk at the park entrance. Before planning to camp at Marble it is a good idea to check on fees, because there are no permanent attendents on duty to give you change. If you have any other problems or questions, a volunteer camp host may be able to help you out. They can usually offer suggestions about the best way to enjoy this scenic area.

As you drive into the campground, watch for a signboard on the right just before the road curves away from the river. Advertisements for interpretive programs are posted here. The covered theatre in the campground is the site for these evening presentations.

Marble has a short season, not opening until mid-June and closing on Labour Day.

Facilities include:
piped water
kitchen shelters
fireboxes
firewood
wheelchair-accessible washrooms
recycling bins
food storage for cyclists
sanitation stations

Backpackers often use Marble Canyon Campground at either end of a backcountry trek. Photo Bob Hahn.

Grizzlies also love the sustenance found on the same avalanche slopes, so stay alert. The only recorded grizzly bear attack in the history of Kootenay National Park occurred at the upper end of the valley.

km 87.4 (7.1)   **Marble Canyon Campground:** Not only is this a very scenic place to camp, it's also an ideal location to mount day expeditions into Banff (it's only half an hour to either Lake Louise or Banff townsite). It's even quite feasible to plan a long day trip up the Icefields Parkway all the way to Athabasca Glacier in Jasper National Park and back again. After mingling with the crowds in Banff, one of Canada's busiest tourist Meccas, it can be a pleasant relief to return to the quieter, more natural confines of Marble Canyon Campground.

If you experience some bad weather, blame it on aptly named Storm Mountain, which is right on the park boundary only 7 km away. But keep in mind that the short self-guided walks at Marble Canyon and the Paint Pots are just about the right length for a rainy day stroll. There is also the possibility of a relatively unknown "wet" adventure in Haffner Canyon, just above the campground (see next entry).

Watch for snowshoe hares around your campsite. There's no better place in the park to see these long-eared bunnies, which really are not rabbits (see page 126). Don't forget to check for an evening program in the theatre. You might learn more about other wildlife in the area, plus a lot of other neat things.

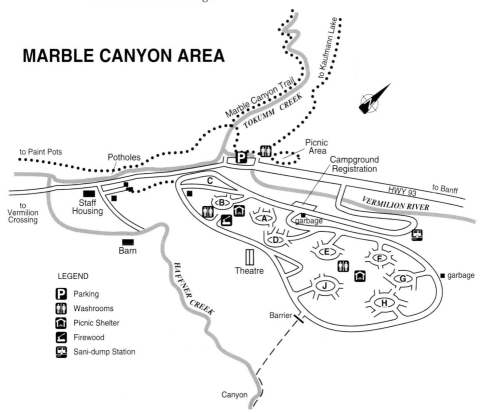

MARBLE CANYON AREA

LEGEND
- **P** Parking
- Washrooms
- Picnic Shelter
- Firewood
- Sani-dump Station

A mix of river beauty and Indian paintbrush brighten the upper reaches of the Vermilion River. Photo Bob Hahn.

Islands of Flowers

As you follow the highway east from Marble Canyon, you may notice patches of lovely pink flowers decorating the banks of the Vermilion River. They are burdened with the lengthy title of broad-leaved willow herb. However, their location makes a more poetic name more appropriate: river beauty. These are little brothers to the taller fireweed, and the flowers are almost the same on both plants. But the flowers on the willow herb are larger and not as numerous.

The broad-leaved willow herb (there is also a dwarf willow herb, but the flowers are only about a centimetre across) loves gravelly places and is quite commonly found on the outwash plain below glaciers. Beds of these pink beauties make a lovely foreground for scenic photos.

The leaves are often used by knowledgable high country hikers to make a tasty salad—but only outside the park. Here, they are only a feast for the eyes.

A Marble Canyon Rescue

As told by Brian Sheehan:

"Only a few days after coming back from my first climbing school, I was called upon to test my newly acquired skills.

"I remember it was a Saturday, and this fellow comes in to say that his St. Bernard had been swept over the falls. We gathered our team together, and found the dog—about 130 feet straight down. He was wrapped around a log, and couldn't move because of the current.

"I rappelled down to the dog with a big pack sack. Wrapping it around him, I tied him in, but it wasn't easy. I was sitting on this wet log, and he was on my lap, and so happy to see me that he kept licking my face and squirming. But we did eventually get the animal up.

"All the time that I had been working, there had been people watching from above, but after the dog was up, they disappeared. I was left on my own to get out of the canyon and that took another 45 minutes."

Brian's first park work was in 1971 as a warden in Saskatchewan's Prince Albert National Park. He became a Kootenay warden in 1974, and was stationed at Marble Canyon.

Haffner Canyon hikers must be prepared to get their feet wet. Photo Bob Hahn.

Haffner Canyon: This canyon has probably been viewed by more snowshoers than warm weather visitors, but it's exciting to view any time of the year. A warning, though: If you really want to explore in the summer, wear an old pair of shoes that won't suffer from a little moisture—well, to be truthful, bootfuls of the wet stuff. Old runners with a little tread left are probably the best choice, because the rocks are slippery.

There are no signs pointing the way to Haffner Canyon, but it's easy to find. Head up the road from the Marble Canyon Campground Theatre until you notice another road to the right. This road has been blocked off by a series of concrete posts set in the ground. Walk between the posts and follow the old road to the banks of Haffner Creek, then turn upstream. You'll soon come upon a covered concrete ring. Located just above that point is a game trail along the creek. If you follow the path, it eventually leads directly to the water. There's no way to avoid a crossing, so give those tootsies a bath.

From here on out it's more of a "way" trail (find the best way) along the rocky streambed, with numerous crossings. If you find the fast-flowing water above your knees and exerting a little more pressure than makes you comfortable, turn around and go back. It won't get any better, and there is no use taking a chance of getting swept away.

However, if you're confident with the crossings—most are easy at normal water levels—continue upstream. You'll notice the farther you go, the narrower the canyon. Notice the "weeping walls." Those drips are the source of the main winter attraction, a magnificent collection of gigantic icicles and other frozen formations. It's no coincidence that the water feels much like liquid ice. Pick a hot day.

Western toads sport a single stripe down their backs.

Warts and All

One of the most surprising wildlife experiences while hiking in the subalpine region is to find your way blocked by a western toad. (There is no need to turn back. Toad attacks are virtually unknown in Kootenay National Park—or anywhere else for that matter.) To those unfamiliar with toad ways, it seems amazing to come upon this rough-skinned amphibian in areas where freezing temperatures are the norm for over half the year. Western toads have been found at elevations as high as 3000 m. Yet, like all amphibians, toads are cold-blooded and generally assume the same temperatures as their surroundings.

Western toads survive in colder climes by correlating daytime activity to altitude. The higher they go, the more active they are when the sun shines. Curiously, they also become lighter coloured at higher elevations. At night, the toads take shelter in a hole of some sort. Often they dig their own. Western toads have been known to burrow 1.3 m deep to hibernate.

Most amphibians are more closely tied to aquatic environments than the western toad is. But special adaptations make life on land easy for the warty creatures. They even have an unusual patch of skin on their stomach that can absorb moisture directly from the ground.

Despite their mostly terrestrial life, toads must migrate to ponds in order to reproduce, just like their relatives. Water is necessary to carry sperm to the eggs and to eventually provide the proper habitat for developing tadpoles. Unfortunately, when the western males gather at the water, they begin to act as unintelligent as they look. They try to mate with anything they can grasp, including other males. But if such an embarrassing thing occurs, the captured male emits a special call. Roughly translated, it means, "Get offa me, you turkey!"

Western toads are big, 55-125 mm long, and they make themselves even larger when attacked. They inflate themselves with air, and stand taller. Their skin is covered with warty-looking glands that produce a mild toxin. This all seems to help. Toads have lived up to 36 years in captivity, and they last longer in the wild than their meager defenses would suggest.

So if you come upon a likely looking candidate for skin treatment, waddling down the trail ahead of you—they walk, instead of hopping—it's almost certain to be the western toad. It won't be moving very fast, and it has a single cream-coloured stripe, which would run from nose to tail if it had a tail. Treat the creature kindly, for its daily menu includes a variety of insects that we probably won't miss, even in a national park.

Finally, there comes a point where the only way to continue upstream is by wading right up the creek. It's not a long slog, because your journey soon ends at a small waterfall. This waterfall is not at all like the thundering torrent in Marble Canyon. You couldn't endure the force of the Marble falls, but brave souls have been known to wade behind the Haffner cascade to explore the mini-cavern located there.

Haffner Canyon is a great adventure on a hot summer day, and you won't find any crowds. Just be sure to watch your step, and **stay cool**.

Vermilion Pass Burn: The dead snags you see towering over the smaller green trees on both sides of the highway are the result of a fire started on July 9, 1968. As with so many fires, this one was ignited by lightning. It burned out of control for three days, until rain came on the fourth day and cooled the blackened hillsides—but not before nearly 2500 ha had burned.

Without a close look, it's easy to say "Tsk, tsk, what a shame," and go on your way, convinced that forest fires should be put out at all costs, because they are so destructive. Parks Canada thought the same way for many years, but the thinking has changed.

Signs of the 1968 Vermilion Pass Burn are obvious, but can anyone deny the beauty of the area? Photo Bob Hahn.

Obviously, a recently burned forest is not a pretty sight, but most newborn babies are none-too-pretty either, no matter what well-meaning friends say. Yet, just like tiny humans, it only takes a few years for a burned mountainside to start showing some beauty and promise of a great future. Take a walk (see the next two entries) and see for yourself.

A group of young hikers nears the end of the hike to Stanley Glacier, the nicest day hike in the park. Photo Bob Hahn.

km 91.0 (3.5)

Stanley Glacier Trailhead: (4.8 km one way, elevation gain 300 m) Ask any Canadian to name the most famous sporting trophy in the country and most will promptly respond, the Stanley Cup. Yet few make the connection between ice hockey's #1 prize and the Stanley Glacier. Along with Stanley Peak and Stanley Creek, it is named after Lord Stanley, an English nobleman who was the sixth governor general of Canada.

The hike to Stanley Glacier is the best day hike in the park for the average visitor. The trip is no hardship for hikers of almost any ability, because the excellent trail has a moderate grade. The scenery is stunning, wildlife sightings are common and a dazzling array of wildflowers usually borders the well-used path.

Like most glaciers in the world, Stanley is receding and is now in sections as you see here. Photo Bob Hahn.

This particular walk has been given the title of "Fire and Ice." The fire part is most obvious, with blackened snags on both sides of the trail and often lying across it. Yet, I defy anyone to declare this an area of devastation. In reality, it is an excellent example of the importance of fire in an ecosystem—a chance for nature to renovate an old worn-out scene and bring in some new actors. But unlike a play, no one can predict the opening night of a forest fire, and there is certainly no script.

One of the catchwords of the last part of the 20th century was biodiversity. It's unfortunate it took so long to recognize the importance of the principles behind the term. We now realize one of the best ways to ensure a wide variety of plants and animals inhabit the environment is through natural changes. Fire is one of the most dramatic ways this can be accomplished.

A dazzling array of wildflowers borders the well-used path. Photo Bob Hahn.

The "Ice" part of the title refers to glacial action, of course (see page 19). The steep slope you traverse in gentle switchbacks was created when a smaller valley glacier (Stanley) was cut off by the larger glacier (Vermilion) that filled the valley where you parked your car. When the trail

This white-tailed ptarmigan is in summer dress. Photo Bob Hahn.

Alpine Chickens

While hiking through a high pass, you may encounter a group of grouse-like birds that don't seem to be any more alarmed by your presence than a flock of chickens might be. Most likely, you've encountered a gang of white-tailed ptarmigan (TAR-mi-gun). To tell them from grouse, look for feathered feet—those on grouse are naked. Also, no matter what time of year it is, the tail is always the colour you would expect on anything named "white-tailed."

In the winter, the tail colour spreads over the entire bird, other than black eyes and beak. Ptarmigan blend so completely with the snow that many cross-country skiers have been shocked to have a drift at their feet explode into cackling feathered projectiles. Summer plumage is a mix of brown and white, also rendering the ptarmigan very well camouflaged. The only break in precedent is during the breeding season, when males sport red eyebrows. The bright colour drives the females wild—or so I've heard.

Of course, like all park wildlife, white-tailed ptarmigan should have no need to fear humans. And they don't. Outside these havens, it's a good thing they live in difficult-to-reach places, or they might go the way of the dodo. Their reluctance to fly is a boon to wildlife photographers, however. I teamed up with a fellow hiker once, to get some great pictures of a female and two chicks. It was simply a matter of my getting into position, and waiting for him to herd the birds in my direction. They never did take to the air.

Swiss Guides in the Rockies

Celebrations in 1999 marked the 100th anniversary of Swiss guides in Canada. The first guides were brought to the country by the Canadian Pacific Railway after mountaineer Philip Stanley Abbot fell to his death near Lake Louise in 1896. Prior to this time, tourist mountaineers had to forge their own routes to the previously unclimbed peaks.

As interest in mountaineering grew, so did the number of Swiss guides. More than 250 first ascents of peaks in the "Canadian Switzerland" are credited to Swiss guides. Their development of safe mountaineering techniques established a basis that still influences modern climbers. They also provided the impetus for the growth of skiing in the Canadian West. Their love of the alpine goes without saying.

Hikers admire the upper end of Stanley Valley from the unofficial lunch stop. Photo Bob Hahn.

levels off, you are entering a hanging valley. Notice the sheer walls of Stanley Peak to your right, a good example of glacial sculpting.

You will eventually come to an area where the forest on the right is different than that on the other side of the trail. The trees, mostly Engelmann spruce mixed with alpine fir, are much larger than any of the living trees seen so far on the hike. For some reason, the fire didn't cross the trail here. You can now see what the forest was like before the fire, and what the young forest in the burned zone will look like again in a couple of hundred years. Whereas lodgepole pine is the dominant species of tree for years after a fire, spruce and fir spring up in the shade of the pines and eventually outnumber them.

Watch for "Stanley" the moose in this section. For many years Stanley and his relatives were often seen browsing on the numerous species of willows that sprang up after the fire. The moose aren't as common now, but look for dark, bulky shapes amidst the grayish-silver snags. You might be lucky.

The other large mammals you are most likely to see on this hike are dark and bulky, too, but not quite as large as moose. Black bears are occasionally seen, especially late in the summer when the grouseberries, strawberries, buffaloberries, blueberries and other sweet fruits ripen. It's a rare treat to see mama black bear and her twin cubs stuffing their faces—at a safe distance, of course.

When the remnants of the mature forest end, a series of stone steps leads up to open talus slopes. As you climb higher, stop and look back. You'll see a textbook example of a U-shaped glacial valley. Also, note another hanging valley on the mountains across the highway.

Eventually, the main trail swings sharply to the left for a short but steep climb to a viewpoint across from the waterfall. This is a good place for lunch. From this point, the trail continues in the direction of the

Climbers on the north ridge of Chimney. Courtesy Parks Canada. Photo Hans Fuhrer.

Climbing in Kootenay

Because virtually all of the mountains in Kootenay are composed of loose limestone and shale, they are not as desirable climbing destinations as the granite spires in nearby areas such as the Bugaboos. One of the main attractions for climbers is that the approaches to the peaks are through true wilderness country. With the exception of the north end of the park, with its high peaks and sheer rock walls, most climbs are only of moderate difficulty.

However, don't take any climb lightly. You are never more than six weeks away from winter, no matter when you come. Be prepared for the unexpected: fog, rain, snow, ice, lightning, stream crossings, animal encounters and more. Hypothermia is an ever-present danger. Weather conditions at the top can be much more severe than in the valley below.

Copies of *The Kootenay Climber's Guide and Mountain Inventory* are available for reference at information centres and the Park Warden headquarters. Volume I contains photographs of the climbing destinations, and Volume II has written descriptions of the routes.

Voluntary Registration

Much of the park is wilderness, and when you venture off the highway a variety of hazards may be encountered. If you are planning an activity you feel is hazardous, we encourage you to leave a detailed itinerary with either family or a friend. If this option is not available, you may choose to complete a Voluntary Safety Registration Form. This will ensure the initiation of a search if you are overdue.

If you register out, you must, by law, register your return. Return the registration card to a park information centre or call the 24-hour phone number listed on the card. Failure to do so may result in an unnecessary and costly search.

Park wardens on a rescue operation. Courtesy Parks Canada. Photo Hans Fuhrer.

glacier for a short distance, officially ending at a yellow trail sign. However, the "unofficial" trail, beyond the sign, leads up to a small treed plateau with an excellent view of Stanley Glacier. Approaching any closer to the glacier is not recommended.

Occasionally, climbers can be seen high on the glacial ice. This activity is not to be attempted by the inexperienced. Many mountaineers register with the wardens before their climb as a safety measure. Then if the climbers don't report back when they are expected, the wardens start checking. Glaciers are dangerous places.

Watch for hoary marmots and pikas (see page 123) amongst the boulders. The much larger, salt-and-pepper-coloured marmots often give away their location by emitting loud whistles. Golden-mantled ground squirrels also range through the rockfields. Some have found the unofficial "picnic area" to be good scrounging, so watch your sandwich.

km 94.5 (0)   **The Continental Divide:** You are now on the spine of western North America. To the west of this point, water flows to the Columbia River and, eventually, to the Pacific Ocean. Raindrops falling on the east side of the Divide reach the Atlantic Ocean via Hudson Bay.

The Divide also marks the boundaries between the provinces of British Columbia and Alberta, and Kootenay and Banff national parks. You might be able to see the forest cuts that mark the border, climbing the mountains on either side of the highway. At intervals, stone cairns or monuments from the early 1900s can be located. Imagine the work it took to mark these boundaries—and helicopters weren't available then.

Here, the Continental Divide not only separates watersheds, but also parks and provinces.

Courtesy Kootenay National Park. Photo Ruth Kihm.

Kootenay's Climber— Hans Fuhrer

Hans was born in Switzerland and grew up to be a stone mason. He also worked as a ski instructor in the winter. His required tour in the Swiss army provided experience in mountaineering and rescue work.

When he was 28, Hans came to Banff to teach skiing. He hadn't planned to stay, but an offer to work in the park was too good to pass up.

"At that time the national parks handled all ski patrols on the hills. There were only two of us at Sunshine, and we had to pack the slopes and watch out for accidents. That was before self-releasing ski bindings, and a lot of falls resulted in breaks—either skis or legs. It was quite different from today, in that there were usually no more than 50 to 100 skiers on the slopes at a time."

Hans left Banff to spend 10 summers as the alpine specialist at the Columbia Icefield in Jasper.

Winters were spent on the ski slopes at Marmot Basin near Jasper. One of the responsibilities of park staff was avalanche control.

"At that time I just carried my pack sack full of dynamite, caps and primer cord. I climbed up the ridges and blasted off cornices. My dad always had dynamite on our little mountain farm, so I wasn't afraid. I always got a big bang out of it."

After Jasper came a stint in Kluane National Park in the Yukon, where he was able to do some expedition climbing in the Mount St. Elias Range. Still, Hans wanted to come back to the Rockies. He eventually accepted an appointment in Kootenay, where he worked until retirement in 1995.

Asked when he started climbing: "Early, hard to say. I grew up in the Alps, and as there was a side hill in the back yard, I automatically started walking up the hill before I knew it was climbing."

Asked about the dangers of climbing:

"Sometimes when I go to climb, the most dangerous stretch is on the highway. If I get hit by a car, that's socially acceptable, but if I'm going to get hit by a rock up in the mountains, people will say, 'Well, that guy wasn't supposed to be up there.'

"Never be too shy to ask somebody when you go into a new area. If I go out on a climb and I don't really know it, I like to ask around to get as much information as I can about the approach, the trails, the river crossings, the conditions, whatever to watch out for.

"I still climb, but maybe not as hard. There are a lot of peaks you like to do over and over because they are classics. But some mountains are too dangerous. You only want to do them once."

While in Kootenay, Hans climbed virtually everything that didn't move, and gradually acquired enough information to write the park's climbing guide.

km 94.5 (0)   **Fireweed Trail:** This self-guiding trail offers a closer look at the burn. It has two routes, with the shorter, lower loop an easy wheelchair accessible 10 minute trip. Beautifully illustrated panels explain what you are actually seeing, and what you probably won't see, depending on the season and your luck at sighting wildlife. Sometimes those critters just don't cooperate, even in a national park. The upper loop (no exhibits) climbs higher into the burn and takes about twice as long to hike.

The name of the trail comes from the tall (up to 1.5 m) plants with spikes of showy pink flowers. Fireweed grows best in disturbed places such as roadsides, and it flourishes in burned areas—which explains its name. The leaves turn such a blazing reddish colour in the fall that imaginative viewers could say the meadows are turned on fire, but that has nothing to do with the name. It's the floral emblem of the Yukon territory.

From the Great Divide it is mostly downhill to Castle Junction (Trans-Canada Highway) from where it is another 30.0 km to Banff. It is 32.0 km to Lake Louise from Castle Junction.

As its name implies, fireweed flourishes in old burns. Photo Bob Hahn.

Wolves rarely present any threat to humans. Photo J. S. Crawford.

The Warden and the Wolves

As told by Darro Stinson:

"One of my most memorable park experiences occurred on a spring day in Jasper. I'd been out for about 10 days along the park boundary, with only my dog for company. Patches of snow still dotted the ground, but the sun was hot and it seemed appropriate to lie down under a tree to take a nap.

"I woke up to a slight growl from my dog. His head was raised and he was looking back down the trail. I looked also, and, not 6 m away, sitting in the rutted path, was a wolf. The dog didn't move, but I sat up, feeling very nervous. Cautiously I glanced around, but could see no other wolves.

"Initially, I felt frightened, but the feeling wore off as I realized that the animal was just curious. It sat there for maybe 15 minutes. When I shifted position, its ears perked up, but that was all.

"Finally, it got up and just started to walk away—and three other wolves rose out of the bush to follow. I hadn't even known they were there.

"Obviously, more sleep was out of the question, so I got up and headed down the trail, reliving the experience in my mind. Then, I paused to look back. Only 20 m behind, four curious wolves followed in my footsteps. Not once did I feel threatened.

"It was one of those very special moments in a person's life."

Darro Stinson is a former superintendent of Kootenay Park. His park career began in 1971 as a truck driver in Banff, but by the end of the season he was a student warden. After graduation from university, he secured a full-time warden position in Jasper. Numerous assignments took him to Newfoundland, Kluane, Nahanni and the Calgary regional office.

A Wildlife Sampler

This magnificent Rocky Mountain bighorn ram enjoys the warmth of a summer day in Kootenay. Photo Bob Hahn.

The wolf's "little brother," the coyote, is often seen along the highway. Photo Bob Hahn.

Animals need Respect

From the Highway

Bighorn sheep, deer, moose, mountain goats, bears—I've seen them all on a single trip through Kootenay National Park without leaving my car. There are no guarantees, but the possibility of seeing any of the park's abundant wild creatures always exists. As is commonly the case, the animals are most active in the mornings or evenings, but midday sightings are not unusual.

The opportunity to see wildlife is one of the most exciting things about visiting a national park. However, upon seeing an animal, many drivers screech to a stop, completely disregarding the traffic rules, to gawk and take photographs. Thus we end up with the infamous "bear jam"—so named because bears are number one on most visitors "must-see" list.

If you come upon a number of cars pulled over to the side of the road, slow down and watch carefully. That's the best way to spot animals, but it also gives you more time to react if some other animal-watcher forgets about traffic. Don't stop unless you can pull completely off the highway. Also, re-member that the best—and safest—chance of photographing the animals is from your vehicle. They are used to seeing cars pass by as opposed to creatures on two feet. Use your car as a movable blind. I've gotten many great wildlife pictures just that way.

How Close is too Close

The main thing to remember is you are the visitor and certain rules of etiquette need to be followed, just the same as if you were a guest in someone's house. If you are on foot, keep reminding yourself, and your family, that these are wild animals, no matter how placid they look. They need their own space and can get very stressed if approached too closely. It's recommended you keep at least three bus lengths away from any large animal—and even farther from bears.

Watch for signs that the animal is getting upset. Examples would be hair standing on end or the stomping of feet. A memorable animal encounter can turn ugly in a hurry if some creature gets agitated. You don't want to get in the way of a heavily hat-racked, 300 kg bull elk when he decides to move. On the other hand, we don't want our creatures so stressed that they need to consult with animal psychiatrists.

If photographing wildlife is one of your priorities, consider buying a large telephoto lens. Then, there is no need to approach your subject too closely. If you really want sharp pictures, be sure to use a tripod. Don't irritate the animals by trying to imitate their calls. You could say the wrong thing and get more of a reaction than you bargained for.

To Feed or Not to Feed

Only one comment should be necessary relative to feeding wild animals in the parks—**DON'T**. It means you are too close and even ground squirrels will bite. They also have ticks that can carry a variety of diseases, from Rocky Mountain spotted fever to bubonic plague.

Your kindness is really not necessary. The animals have an abundance of natural food in the summer and don't need our junk food. Even we don't need our junk food!

Visitors can easily see wildlife in their local zoos, but seeing a confined creature is not the same as observing it in the wild. And animals in the park that get used to handouts aren't really wild anymore. So always say **No!** to moochers.

A Note on Bears

Bears need special mention, because there are so many misconceptions about them. The main thing is to treat bears with respect and use common sense in their terrain. The best way to avoid problems with bears is to avoid them—it's not smart to take chances.

When you are camping, hiking or backpacking, follow the precautions listed in this section. There is no guarantee sticking to these rules will prevent bear problems, but the chance of an encounter is greatly reduced. Bears are individuals and react differently—just like people—but having some guidelines to follow only makes good sense.

Many backcountry users now carry pepper spray to be used as a possible deterrent to bears. However, just like any of the other suggestions for dealing with bears, the spray is not a sure thing. Read the directions carefully and hope you never have to follow them. Pepper spray is something to be used as a last resort in an emergency, not as a guarantee of safety.

Bear Encounters

If you meet a bear on the trail:

– Stop, stand quietly and don't look the animal in the eyes.
– Watch the bear out of the corner of your eye and back up slowly.
– Try to determine whether you are facing a grizzly or black bear.*
– If the bear doesn't seem aggressive and you get out of its sight, leave the area as quickly as you can, but do not run.

If the bear charges:

Stand your ground and hope the charge is a bluff.

If a black bear is definitely going to make contact:

Yell, wave your arms, throw rocks, punch, kick and fight with all your might. Black bears can often be driven away. Lying still often encourages them to treat you as prey.

If a grizzly bear is definitely going to make contact:

– Drop to the ground—stomach down, legs spread.
– Leave your pack on for extra protection.
– Lock your hands behind your neck, arms close to your head.
– Remain immobile no matter what happens. Grizzlies attack mainly to intimidate and will usually end an attack when you show submission. They rarely treat humans as prey.
– Never run away. You can't outrun a bear.

* If it is black, fight back!—If it has a hump, be a lump!

How Many Bears

Just like with the wolves, visitors are always curious about the number of bears in the park. That's one of the mysteries researchers hoped to solve during a five-year cooperative bear study, directed by Dr. Bruce McLellan and Dr. John Woods, which began in 1994. The West Slopes Bear Research Project was also designed to learn more about bear survival rates and their sources of mortality, as well as identifying suitable habitat both inside and outside national parks. Information on key movement corridors was also collected. (A sister study, the Eastern Slopes Grizzly Bear Project, was conducted at the same time.)

The usual way to study bear ecology is to catch the animals in cable snares—the cables are padded to prevent serious injury—before tranquillizing them, so that they can be weighed, measured and have a small premolar tooth removed for aging. Blood samples are also taken. On occasion, tags and ribbons may be attached for visual identification.

Then, before the bear is released, it is fitted with a radio collar. The radio collars are guaranteed for five years, but often work longer. In recent studies, a pair of ear transmitters was substituted for the collar. The maximum life for the transmitters is two years—and then only if they shut down at night. But by programming one transmitter to turn on at the end of the other's life, researchers can track for at least four years.

As part of the West Slopes Study, tissue and hair samples were taken from captured bears. Along with the blood, they provided a DNA "fingerprint" for each animal. Hair samples were regularly collected at strategically-located sampling stations—strands of barbed-wire wound around trees saturated with fish fertilizer. By analyzing the hair and collected bear scat, the movement of individual bears could be traced. This pioneering research not only aids in determining bear numbers, it also supplies clues as to the genetic health of the population.

Bear research is a paradox. No-one knows how traumatic it is for a bear to be captured and collared, but it's for their own good. (Compare that to your last trip to the dentist.) Hopefully, the new technology will reduce the need to collar bears, but it can't completely replace the traditional tools. Too bad, for as Kootenay's chief warden, Paul Galbraith states, "I'd like to know that there is at least one grizzly out there who isn't wearing a radio collar."

By using radio collars or ear transmitters, researchers can track the movements of bears.

Warden John Niddrie prepares to tranquillize a problem bear. Photo Bob Hahn.

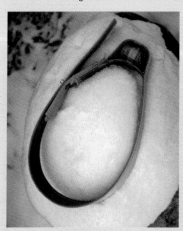 

The *Horrible Bear?*

"Horrible bear"—that's the label Lewis and Clark hung on the grizzly, when they first encountered the animals during their expedition to western North America (1804-1806). The name was even adopted by biologists, who gave grizzlies the scientific name of *Ursus horribilis.* Most sources now use the name *Ursus arctos.*

Unfortunately, too many park visitors are still convinced the "horrible" adjective is quite appropriate for the largest of North America's mountain carnivores. It's reflected in comments such as, "I would never stay in a tent because of the bears." Many of our visitors would place the hump-backed bears in the same category as werewolves, boogeymen or aliens from outer space. And humans have always harbored a fear, usually unreasonable, of the unknown.

I'm always leery of anyone who reports a grizzly sighting. Many people still believe any bear that isn't black must be a grizzly. Actually, the prettiest grizzly I ever saw was black! However, the black hairs were tipped with white, which gives rise to the nickname "silvertip." Unlike black bears, grizzlies are seldom a solid colour.

There is rarely good reason to stay off the trails in Kootenay National Park for fear of encountering a grizzly (but never ignore bear warnings or trail closures). In more than a decade in the park, I have seen only one griz—and it was alongside the highway! During the entire 20th century only one case of grizzly-caused human injury in the park was recorded.

However, you should learn all you can about bears—be sure and read the park publications—and

The large shoulder hump and dished-in face identifies this as a grizzly bear.

follow the suggestions for camping and travel in bear country.

If you feel more information is needed, pick up almost any book about outdoor activities in the Canadian Rockies and you'll find page after page devoted to bears and bear encounters.

One of the most exciting things about hiking in the park is the knowledge the bears are out there, whether you see them or not. Just the anticipation of seeing a bear can prompt a minor adrenalin rush. I don't intentionally go looking for thrills when I hike—unlike the people who engage in activities like sky diving or bungee jumping. My little thrill comes from knowing a grizzly could be just around the corner. I don't worry about it—chances are it would be gone before I see it, anyhow—but I am alert and prepared.

Kootenay is bear country, but use common sense and hike without fear. You are safer on the park trails than on the highway or in many large cities. In all probability, our hairy four-legged beasts won't give you as much trouble as some of your smooth-skinned, smooth-talking,two-legged neighbours.

Although classed as carnivores, bears feed primarily on plants. Photo Bob Hahn.

they have a different profile. A line drawn from the forehead of a black bear to the end of its nose would be almost straight, whereas the griz has an indentation in between. Thus, a grizzly's nose seems to turn up like a warped ski jump. Grizzlies also have much larger front claws than their cousins, but you'd probably have to get too close to see the difference.

One of the best times of the year to view black bears is in the early summer when there is a proliferation of dandelions along the roadsides. One June day I watched a yearling black bear gobbling dandelion heads for over an hour near the Kootenay River. The youngster spooked occasionally when a large truck roared by, but was soon back swallowing flowers.

However, in the early '90s, park biologists began to wonder if sights such as that described above could become less common. Some studies have hinted at the possibility populations of bears in Kootenay and the other Rocky Mountain parks were declining. With the grizzly's propensity for solitude and space, it's understandable that as more and more visitors flock to the national parks, the bears would be affected. But even the more sociable black bears—common in so much of the province—seemed to be responding to increased human pressure in the parks.

Outside parks, human populations are increasing and bears, which wander widely, are likely to come to grief in these areas. For the sake of the animals, it's important to convince the human residents of bear country to change some of their habits, especially those related to garbage disposal.

A Bear for All People

While grizzly bears reign as the aristocrats of the Rocky Mountain bear community, black bears form the *hoi polloi,* the commoners. They don't need as much space as grizzlies do, and they are more tolerant of people. Thus almost any bear, regardless of colour, that you see along the highway in Kootenay Park will be a black bear. I say ignore the colour, because black bears come in about every shade but chartreuse. There have been no sightings of blue or white bears in the park, but some can be found in other parts of British Columbia. And they all come under the heading of "black bear."

In actual fact, you will rarely see a black bear in the Canadian Rockies that isn't either a solid black or brown (cinnamon) colour. Quite commonly, they will also have a white "V" on their chests that can only be seen when the bears stand erect, something that doesn't happen very often.

Black bears lack the large shoulder hump of mature grizzlies, and

Cat of Many Names

When you hike along the Juniper trail or any of the other dry areas in the south end of the park, be aware that you're in lion country. There have been more mountain lion sightings in this area of the park than any other. These cats of many names (puma, cougar, painter, catamount…) are found where their prey—usually deer—is most numerous. However, like most predators they are opportunists and prey on a variety of animals, including bighorn sheep. As most of the park's bighorns (150-175) winter around Radium Hot Springs, some cats have developed a preference for mutton instead of venison.

Most of the mountain lion sightings in Kootenay have been at the southern end. Photo Bob Hahn.

It's not necessary to keep looking over your shoulder, though, because cougars rarely come after people, especially adults. Most attacks on humans in North America have been small children, when the cat was obviously hungry, but those cases are also rare. If cougar attacks were common they wouldn't get so much publicity. The big cats are more likely to come after a small dog (see page 48)—almost as if exacting revenge for years of canine harassment of the cougar's domestic cousins. You're not even likely to see a mountain lion—I've seen only two in over a third of a century of wandering the wild country. One of these was face-to-face near the Simpson River, when I was on my knees photographing wildflowers. It was rather exciting, to say the least.

If you see a cougar, you can't mistake it for anything else. The big giveaway is the plump, black-tipped tail that makes up about one-third of the cat's 1.8 to 2.5 m length. Most males weigh in at 63 to 72 kg, while females average 40 to 50 kg. The all-time record is 125 kg, a trophy taken by former U.S. president and avid hunter Teddy Roosevelt.

In most areas, cougars prey mainly on deer; in Kootenay they seem to prefer mutton. Photo Bob Hahn.

Canine Travellers—Wolves of the Rockies

Curious visitors frequently ask, "How many wolves do you have in the park?" That's a simple, direct question, but the answer isn't quite as straightforward. Let's consider the case of Pluie, even though she probably never set foot in Kootenay National Park.

Pluie was a five year-old female who was trapped in Kananaskis Country, east of Banff. Researchers worked through a rainstorm to fit the wolf with a radio collar. As the French word for rain is pluie, the name was a natural.

Pluie turned out to be a great traveller. Before long she trotted all the way down to Montana. Later, she wandered back north to Banff, but Montana still beckoned and once more Pluie headed south of the border. This time her explorations took her over the mountains and she returned to Canada on the British Columbia side of the Rockies. Pluie came as far north as Canal Flats (about 50 km south of the village of Radium Hot Springs) where she met a male wolf. By an amazing coincidence, the male, Orion, also had a radio-collar,

Wolves have been persecuted for years, even in our national parks. Photo Bob Hahn.

which he had gotten in Kootenay—maybe that's what attracted Pluie. Pluie and Orion became a pair and they travelled up the Findlay Creek drainage to raise a family. Unfortunately, there is no happy ending to the story. As is too often the case, both wolves were later killed by a hunter.

During a period of three years Pluie covered an area of over 100,000 km^2 (she was tracked by satellite). Kootenay National Park is less than 1500 km^2 and Yoho is even smaller. Most wolves may not travel as much as Pluie, but some have gone even farther. With their long legs they can easily cover 75 km in a day.

How can we determine the number of wolves in Kootenay when the elusive canids come and go at will? Our wolves, if we can call them that, are part of a larger population that stretches from Jasper, and points north, all the way to Interstate Highway 190 in southern Montana. In an effort to maintain a viable population of wolves in the ecosystem, the Central Rockies Wolf Project—directed by Carolyn Callaghan and Cam McTavish—was initiated in 1987, with Parks Canada as a partner.

The encroachment of civilization on traditional travel routes of the wide-ranging wolves is a major factor in limiting populations. Wolves are montane animals who shun high mountain passes in favour of the valley floors—the areas of major development, even in our national parks. These are the main transportation corridors and the highways and railroads often become death traps for wildlife, including the normally shy wolf clan. Winters are the worst time, because wolves seek out paths cleared

through the snow, as any sensible human would do, but they are no match for our high-powered machines. During the winter of 1998-99, the deaths of five wolves were recorded in Yoho National Park. Only one died a natural death—three wolves were killed on the railroad and another on the highway. This mortality decimated the Yoho wolf pack.

In the mid-1990s, newspaper headlines all over the world proclaimed: "Wolves Reintroduced to Yellowstone." And, as the wolves came from Canada, it simply perpetuated the idea our wolves abound and have been around forever, especially in our mountain parks. In actual fact, wolves were virtually eliminated from Canada's Rocky Mountain parks twice during the last century.

Wolf control began early in the 1920s, primarily owing to the Victorian attitude that predators—read meat-eaters—were bad and vegetarians were good. Thus war was declared not only on wolves, but also on coyotes, cougars, lynx, weasels and an assortment of other unfortunate carnivores. In the 1940s, wolf populations began to rebound only to be faced by another crisis—a rabies scare. The war commenced anew. It wasn't until the winter of 1982-83, after an absence of 30 years, that reliable sightings of wolves in Kootenay were reported once again.

Throughout the 1990s, researchers estimated the Kootenay pack numbered from seven to nine individuals most of the time. Yet, much of what we know about the wolves in Kootenay comes from a radio-collared duo that were both classified as loners. Amber, a nine year-old female named for her striking eye colour, broadcasted signals for almost six years. Topaz,

My first sighting of a reclusive Kootenay wolf. Photo Bob Hahn.

a male, left the park several times as might be expected when Kootenay's population of elk, the wolves' favourite prey, is only a tenth of what it used to be. Both animals are now off the air.

The researchers, plus volunteers and park personnel, garner most of their information during the wintertime, when snow cover reveals some of the wolves' activities as plainly as if they were recorded on paper. The scientists go out of their way not to disturb the animals, rarely getting close enough to see them. Tracking is generally done in the opposite direction from that which the wolves are travelling, so there are no chance encounters. Lots of ski time is spent locating the leftovers from dinner, where samples are taken from the prey to determine species, age and physical condition.

Tracking wolves may sound glamorous, but, like most research, it's not very exciting most of the time. I have to give credit to those dedicated people doing their gruelling best to ensure carnivores like the wolf are around for years to come. I'm thrilled by the bone-chilling howl of a wolf pack, but the sound has to be doubly satisfying to the folks who call wolves by their first names.

Battling bighorn rams can't help but give each other headaches. Photo Bob Hahn.

Battered Bighorns

After entering the West Gate, the first large animals most visitors see are brownish-grey Rocky Mountain bighorn sheep (goats are white). One of the first questions that comes to mind is, "If these are bighorn sheep, how come they have little horns?" There's a good reason. The majority of sheep seen along the highway are females (ewes) and their lambs. Only the adult males, or rams, have massive snail-shell like horns.

When you do see a mature bighorn ram, there will no longer be any doubt as to the accuracy of the name. But take a closer look at the sober-faced stocky animals. Notice the Roman noses on some. Maybe you can even see some old facial scars. These are definitely battered animals! But no one has abused them. The battering comes from their own hands...er horns.

Broken noses and other scars are medals of battle and stem from head-on combat the rams engage in during the months of November and December. That is mating time,

as you might imagine, and, as with most animals—including the human kind—males go to considerable lengths to garner the favours of an attractive female. In the case of bighorns, an initial effort is made to avoid any violent jousting, by posing and posturing. In effect, the larger rams say to the youngsters, "Take a good look, kid. You mess with me and these horns will make mutton outa ya."

However, when two amorous rams are fairly equal in size, combat may be the only way to settle things. First, the pair may stand side by side, although facing opposite directions, and slash at each other with their hooves. This is accompanied by an unmelodious assortment of snorts and grunts. These actions are just a warm-up for the main event. That involves backing off a dozen or so metres, rearing up on their hind legs with front legs churning, before lunging forward, head foremost, to smash together with a resounding crack. Ever wonder about the phrase "battering ram"? Now you know where it comes from.

After the rams return to earth, they are both undoubtedly seeing stars. But thanks to an abnormally thick skull, they soon regain their senses (some people may question my choice of words), and are ready to "meet" again. This combat may go on from dawn to dusk, or even longer, until one of the duellists has had his bell rung so many times he must feel like the Winchester Cathedral belfry. Then the loser just wanders off, all thoughts of passion having been literally knocked out of his head. Unfortunately, even the winner may also turn out to be a loser when he looks for his ewe, only to find some other ram has slipped off with his anticipated "prize" during the battle.

Billy, Nanny and the Kids

The mountain goat is the symbol of Kootenay National Park. Photo Bob Hahn.

The symbol of Kootenay National Park is the mountain goat. Up to 300 of the white climbers can be found on the steep alpine slopes in the park. Most of the time nobody gets too worked up about mountain goats, mainly because they are rarely seen without the use of binoculars. To the casual long-distant observer, the animal's apparently hum-drum lifestyle makes them appear about as exciting as furry high-altitude cows. In reality, mountain goats are far from placid, with a complex social structure that would be enough to turn the healthiest of humans into milk-swigging, ulcer-plagued wrecks.

About the only time most people see mountain goats up close is when the animals venture down to licks near the highway. There is a hint of unrest, but that is to be expected. The animals are nervous about being so close to humans and their noisy machines, but they are equally apprehensive about being so close to each other! High in their alpine haunts mountain goats are rarely seen in large herds, because the white beasts are downright antisocial. If one goat gets within a few metres of another, look for trouble. There could be a fight!

Mountain goats probably "fight" more than any other large mammals, but they aren't given credit for their pugnacious behaviour. The headliners in the park are bighorn sheep. The ram's head-smashing escapades are known far and wide, but the duels only take place during the fall mating season. Mountain goats squabble all year round. But if they engaged in the same head-to-head combat as the bighorns, they would have ceased to exist long ago. Their short, black stiletto-like horns are capable of inflicting terrible puncture wounds. There are even a couple of recorded cases where grizzly bears came out second-best in goat encounters.

Most mountain goat conflicts involve a lot of posturing, but few injuries. The accepted position for a battle is head-to-rump with the combatants doing a lot of circling. Thus, if an animal does get punctured, the wound is usually in its hind quarters. The hide in the rump area is actually thicker than anywhere else on the body. However, most disagreements never reach head-to-rump stage. One goat usually shows displeasure through a variety of body posturings like raising its hair, arching its back or stamping its feet. Then the antagonist usually backs off.

This antisocial behavior is actually vital to mountain goat survival. From a distance, most goat ranges look very barren. Yet, there has to be enough of the grasses and sedges that goats prefer, along with a variety of other plants, or the animals wouldn't be there. But the lush meadows found at lower elevations are rare. Vegetation is scattered all over the slopes and so are the goats. Large herds could soon overgraze an area. The white climber's intolerance of each other keeps this from happening.

Wide dispersal of the goats also helps to ensure their survival in a more direct way. The number of mountain goats who die in avalanches is probably greater than those killed by any other natural cause. But a single avalanche will never catch more than a few of the scattered beasts at a time.

Did you ever wonder why any creature would choose to live in an environment where food is scarce, avalanches common and one wrong step could be fatal (goats do slip, but not very often)? One look at a mountain goat in its winter coat, with hair up to 20 cm long, should tell you they are designed for cold weather. The heavy fur is shed every summer, but hot days are still hard to take. A mountain goat's body temperature is higher than ours and they don't even have pores or sweat glands to get rid of excess heat. No wonder these holdovers from the ice age

Even the kids instinctively know that the proper fighting position is head to rump. Photo Bob Hahn.

choose to live on the rugged alpine slopes amongst the glaciers and snow patches.

Mountain goats don't spend all of their time scrambling about on sheer cliffs. Food is usually more plentiful in the level places. But you can be sure they don't stay put very long. At the first sign of danger the animals race to the nearest precipice and climb to impossibly tiny ledges. That certainly stops anyone foolish enough to be pursuing the goats including virtually every creature that might entertain the thought of a goat dinner. The only large predator that can manoeuvre on at least some sections of the goat's escape terrain is the cougar, but the cats are not a great hazard. In fact, there isn't a single animal that depends on mountain goats for food.

Mountain goats have no equal in the world (they aren't really goats at all). Actually, the entire population of 80,000 is found only in North America, with almost two-thirds of that number in British Columbia alone. And the white climbers still flourish in the same rugged mountain heights they populated thousands of years ago. Few large mammals have been less affected by the advances of civilization.

But even the most remote places may not be safe in our modern world. Mountain goat populations have declined in a number of areas after roads were pushed in. Hunters probably took the greatest toll in these cases—goats rely too much on their climbing ability for safety rather than concealment like most animals—but regulations permitted it. In a world where we have exterminated so many natural predators, hunters must often assume the role of wolves and moun-

Heavy winter coats must be shed each summer, prompting some visitors to report seeing "sick" goats. Photo Bob Hahn.

tain lions to help control populations of animals like deer. But mountain goats don't need hunter-aided population controls. The belligerent beasts regulate their own population just by being antisocial individuals who live in an unforgiving environment.

However, the goat populations of southeastern British Columbia mysteriously declined in the late 1990s. Biologists have yet to determine the exact reason, but are guessing a combination of factors, from bad winters to human pressure, are to blame. If the numbers are down in Kootenay Park, as suspected, it would indicate human factors other than hunting have more effect than we realize. More research is needed.

The mountain goat is a fitting symbol for Kootenay National Park. These hardy mountaineers have survived in the face of adversity for thousands of years and should continue to do so, especially within special protected areas. All hail the mountain goat and Kootenay National Park—partners in perpetuity.

Moose are the largest members of the deer family. Even a small one is big. Photo Bob Hahn.

Winner by a Nose —the Moose

If the shape of a nose has anything to do with social standing, moose have to be one of the leading aristocrats. They definitely have the most distinctive nose of all the ungulates in the park. Their noses are similar to those of horses, but that's like saying turkeys look like peacocks.

Moose are the largest members of the deer family—easily as large as most horses (maximum weight in the park for males is about 450 kg). Even small moose are big. Moose are the simplest members of the deer family to identify, with their long legs and deep brown to black body. However, I once watched one at a distance, whose hind legs looked like parallel white lines. But there was no light-coloured rump patch like those found in all of the moose's smaller relatives. There never is.

Moose antlers are unique in having flattened palms. As with other antlered animals (antlers drop off each year; horns are permanent), antler size increases annually until old age takes its toll. Then the antlers decrease in size. Males also have a skin-like growth hanging down from the throat area, called the bell, whose length can increase as the bulls grow older. However, it's an unreliable method of determining age. The more winters the animal has seen, the more likely there's been one cold enough to freeze off his bell.

Moose are seen most often in the Kootenay and Vermilion River valleys, but they aren't common anywhere in the park. Check out the roadside licks, but if you see one of the giant deer, don't get too close.

Like many other animals, moose seem to be the most dangerous when either sex or babies are involved. I've heard more than one experienced outdoorsman say they would rather face a grizzly than an irate mother moose with calf. In the fall, bulls are the most aggressive. Their hormones can drive them to attack almost anything that moves or makes strange noises. During the rut (mating season), big bulls wander around uttering love calls, also taken as challenges by other males. The call is a guttural grunting.

Ordinarily moose don't respond to grunts until at least mid-September in the park area. However, there are exceptions, as I learned one August day on the Stanley Glacier trail. When I grunted at a lone bull, he immediately raised his head and started in my direction. No damage was done, but there was a lesson to be learned: keep the grunts to yourself in moose country.

Hello, Deer

Members of the deer family are a common sight in the Kootenay River valley. White-tailed and mule deer are the most common, and, some would say, the only deer in the park. This isn't so! Those two species are actually the smallest members of the deer clan in Kootenay, which also includes elk and moose. All members of the deer family have cloven hooves. Also, the males grow new antlers every year. As a point of interest, there is a fifth member of the deer family where both sexes sport antlers. These mountain caribou are not found in Kootenay, but Jasper National Park has them.

Antler structure is different in all five species, but most of the animals you see don't have coat racks on their heads, so look rumpward. Only the moose is lacking a light-coloured posterior—and looking at back ends is the easiest way to distinguish between mule deer, white-tails and cow elk. Getting a good look is usually no problem, because the tail end is the last thing you see before they disappear into the forest.

Elk are larger than mule deer or white-tails, and have a large beige-coloured patch on their rump. Ben Gadd* describes the shape as being like that of a light bulb. The tiny tail is the same colour as the rest of the patch.

Both white-tailed and mule deer have white patches on their rumps, but, surprisingly, the white colour is much more noticeable on a mulie than a white-tail—as long as the tail is down. But when a white-tail raises its big white semaphore, there's no question of how they got their name. The mulie's tail is much smaller in comparison and has a black tip.

Watch carefully as a white-tailed deer runs off—that's what usually happens right after the flag goes up—and you'll see they move as horses do. They have evolved for running in open country. In sharp contrast, mule deer employ a comical stiff-legged bounce, moving like

Top: The big beige rump patch and large antlers identify a mature bull elk. Photo Bob Hahn.

Bottom: Elk are frequently preyed upon by wolves in the winter. Nothing remains but bones. Photo Bob Hahn.

121

Top: This mule deer, still in velvet, always displays a prominent white rump patch. Photo Bob Hahn.

Bottom: It's hard to understand where the white-tail deer gets its name until the large tail is raised. Photo Bob Hahn.

animated pogo sticks. Their speciality is jumping to safety in deep, log-strewn forests.

In the park, white-tails are concentrated primarily along the Kootenay River up to Kootenay Crossing. They rarely winter in the park; most migrate down the Kootenay River valley. Years ago, white-tails were outnumbered in the park by mule deer, but the white-tail population has been steadily increasing.

Mule deer range higher than their flag-waving cousins, with some of the larger bucks even enjoying the summer sights of alpine country. I surprised six one day while searching for mountain goats to photograph. Mulies can be found all through the park, but they are probably most numerous in the southern end of the Kootenay River valley, like the white-tails. However, when the snow starts to pile up, they usually migrate to southwest-facing slopes in the Columbia Valley.

Winter is a critical time for grazing animals as well as the creatures that prey on them such as mountain lions. The number of deer taken by predators in the winter may increase, but it is only a small percentage of total fatalities. Too many are killed by motor vehicles, so obey speed limits and drive carefully. Slow down whenever you see a deer near the highway. You never know what it's going to do. Some deer are almost as unpredictable as some people.

*Handbook of the Canadian Rockies

Who Goes There?

Those miniature sentinels you see standing atop their burrows alongside the highway near McLeod Meadows are Columbian ground squirrels, not traffic monitors. And their posts are not just limited to the roadsides. In fact, they can be found almost anywhere in the park, from the lawn of the administration building to the highest alpine meadow.

Columbians are the largest of the animals we commonly call ground squirrels (often mistakenly called gophers), growing to 30 cm in length, with another 8 to 12 cm of bushy tail. At higher altitudes they might be mistaken for hoary marmots, because both creatures have mottled gray upper parts. However, the squirrel is much smaller, and has rufous feet (marmot's feet are black) and legs, as well a reddish-brown nose. The marmots emit a loud, high-pitched whistle, while the Columbian ground squirrel produces a chirp that, while not as loud as a marmot's call, is still so vigourous it makes its whole body quiver.

When not looking for intruders, squirrels forage for a variety of vegetarian food. They feed ravenously for only about four months, then hibernate the rest of the year. One unusual aspect of their hibernation is the ground squirrels at the lowest elevations disappear underground to sleep as early as mid-August, while alpine-zone ones might not go to bed until October. As you would expect, ground squirrels in the valleys also emerge earlier in the spring than their high country relatives.

Top: Columbian ground squirrels, like these youngsters, are often wrongly called "gophers."

Middle: Hoary marmots are larger than ground squirrels with a salt and pepper colour and black feet.

Bottom: Golden-mantled ground squirrels are often mistaken for chipmunks.

Photos Bob Hahn.

123

Haymaker of the Heights

Pikas are related to rabbits and hares, but they were shortchanged when it came to ears. Photo Bob Hahn.

A hike in alpine country is an adventure like no other. It's a journey to another world where gigantic peaks tower over miniature alpine flowers. Often, another miniature of the high country can be seen gathering the flowers and carrying them back to the boulder fields where it lives. This furry, chinchilla-like creature is called the pika.

Pikas can be gray or grayish-brown and are about the size and shape of guinea pigs, but they aren't rodents. A quick survey of facial features shows the similarity to their nearest relatives, the rabbits and hares. In fact, pikas are sometimes called rock rabbits. However, they've been shortchanged when it comes to ears, and there is no sign of a fluffy white tail or any other kind of tail.

The pika's ears don't flop in the breeze like a rabbit's, because they are short and rounded. It's a good thing, because pikas don't hibernate and you'd think long ears might freeze off during the severe mountain winters. Actually, the animals remain protected under an insulating blanket of snow. Yet, pikas still have to keep moving in the near-freezing environment. They haven't accumulated an extra layer of stored fat like the snoring marmots next door.

In order to have enough energy to remain active year-round, pikas must spend late summer and fall "making hay." They gather not only flowers, but virtually any kind of vegetation they can find and then spread the plants out on boulders to dry. These hay piles can be up to two feet high. Some of the hay is later stored under the rocks for winter grub.

It is facinating to watch these tiny creatures at work. I'm still trying to get a photograph of one scampering (they lack the rabbit's long hind legs for hopping) over the talus slopes with a yard-long stalk of fireweed clenched in its teeth. But when pikas are harvesting they rarely stop to pose.

Fortunately for our North American pikas, their boulder field homes offer more security than the domains of some Asiatic relatives called Daurian pikas. (Twelve of the 14 species of pikas are found in Asia.) These burrow-dwellers of the Gobi desert grasslands can be so plentiful that a single square mile may contain up to 1000 hay piles. The hay is easy picking for Mongolian herdsman who often bring their livestock to pilfer from the hard-working pika's winter stores.

Pikas are most aggressive during harvest-time because the hay is so critical to their survival. That's when you often see one gray bundle racing after another. The chase continues until the intruder is clear of the occupant's territory. Then, just like in some real-life cartoon, the action suddenly reverses and the pursuer becomes the pursued. Very little aggression is displayed in May or early June during mating or a month later when the two to five young are born. This lack of aggression is rare in the animal kingdom where an excess of sex hormones causes so many strange things: hummingbirds attacking eagles, bull moose challenging freight trains and bighorn sheep trying to knock each other's blocks off.

New-born pikas are lightly furred and have both eyes and ears closed. About a week after birth they begin to call and walk unsteadily. Incredibly, they are weaned in less than two weeks and attain full size of 6-8 inches and 4-6 ounces in only 40 or 50 days. This extremely rapid growth is necessary, because each animal has to establish a territory and start making hay long before the snow begins to fall. In addition, females often have a second litter—but these young rarely survive.

As you might imagine, a plump little animal like the pika makes a tasty mouthful for predators. But, because they live in loose colonies, there is usually one set of eyes to spot any hungry intruder and sound the warning call. These calls vary—in the Rockies the sound is a weak "eek," somewhat like a sickly lamb with a lisp. However, pikas of the Sierra Nevadas make a sharp rasping bark.

The amount of noise depends on the type of predator. Warnings are quickly sounded whenever an eagle or hawk flies overhead or a large mammal approaches. Then the pikas scamper into the complex of passageways under the boulders where their larger enemies can't follow. However, when a weasel appears there are no warning cries. As if knowing that any sign of their presence could be fatal, the pikas silently steal away.

Pika hay dries in the sun before being stored under the rocks. Photo Bob Hahn.

Of course, pikas know humans can't slither under the rocks and are quick to sound off when we appear. Unfortunately, they are excellent ventriloquists, so it is difficult to figure out exactly where the cries are coming from. Thus, the only way to locate the animals is to scan as much of the boulder field as possible, and when one of the rocks moves—there's the pika.

Pikas are hardest to approach in the spring, but this is only logical when you consider they have just emerged from months spent in a dark, silent world under the rocks and snow. Upon emergence they are not only assailed by strange new sounds, but open spaces don't offer the same protection as the confines of a narrow tunnel.

I think pikas are great little animals. To me, any sighting of the dimunitive creatures makes a high mountain trek more memorable. I am even willing to overlook the pika's distasteful habit of eating their own droppings in the winter. However, they only eat the soft, green pellets composed of partially digested food, not regular droppings. Doesn't that make you feel better?

Top: Lynx are rare in the park.

Bottom: Snowshoe hares retain their white snowshoes year-round.

Photos Bob Hahn.

Predator and Prey

Do rabbits turn white in winter to match the snow, or do they turn white even without any snow? The correct answer is neither of the above. Only hares change colour. Snowshoe hares are the only long-eared hoppers you're likely to see in the park. They have fuzzy white coats in the winter and white snowshoes year-round.

Snowshoe hares can be found anywhere in the park, but I've seen more in the Marble Canyon area than anywhere else. However, sightings were rare between 1992 and 1995. Populations of hares in North America seem to fluctuate in cycles of approximately nine years,

and the years mentioned were obviously a low point in the cycle. The population has recovered and no wonder—females are capable of having up to four litters a year with a maximum of eight little bunnies each. The average is two to four.

Besides the colour changes, hares differ from rabbits in another way. They don't dig dens or build nests. The young are born in an unlined depression in the ground, fully furred with their eyes open. If they were naked and blind at birth, like their cottontail cousins, few would survive.

The survival rates for hares is not very high to begin with, because virtually every predator finds them extremely tasty. In Kootenay, snowshoe hares are pursued by a variety of birds, weasels and members of both the dog and cat families.

Throughout most of the snowshoe hare's northern range, the chief predators are lynx. From 60-90 per cent of a lynx's diet may consist of snowshoes. They are so dependent on hares that when the population of bunnies drops, a decline in lynx typically follows.

Ongoing research directed by Clayton Apps has shown this is marginal habitat for lynx. Yet, the Vermilion Pass Burn should be ideal. It contains both the open spaces the cats need for hunting and dense forest nearby to raise their families. But the population isn't increasing despite an abundance of hares.

One characteristic of lynx that enables them to run down the hares are snowshoes of their own. The heavily-furred paws are almost the same size as those of a cougar, but look 6 times as large. They also have grayish-beige coats and long black ear tufts.

It's just too bad lynx can't multiply like snowshoe hares.

Old Brown Eyes

Visitors to Redstreak Campground are occasionally surprised to find a large, brown-eyed owl observing them from a nearby tree—barred owls can see very well in the day-time. Lacking the glaring yellow orbs of most owls—only four of the 18 owls native to North America have brown eyes—this owl appears to be a gentle creature. And its demeanor lives up to its appearance. They are easily approached and will even tolerate humans close to their nests. Neither human presence nor voices seem to bother them.

Barred owls prefer the same old-growth forest as the endangered spotted owls and probably aid in their demise by usurping territories of the smaller owls along the West Coast. The fourth largest of North American owls, barred owls are exceeded in size only by the snowy, great horned and great gray owls. The latter two species are uncommon permanent residents of Kootenay as are the rest of the owls. Most common in the park along with the great horned owl are smaller owls such as the boreal, northern pygmy and northern saw-whet.

A Most Unmusical Bird

Quoth the raven, "Nevermore," wrote Edgar Allan Poe in his famous poem. Poets tend to exaggerate, but the "awks" and other guttural cries that ravens emit seem to be far removed from any human tongue. It's even hard to accept the fact that the raven is the largest songbird, order *Passeriformes*.

Ravens are large, black crow-like birds that you often see on the shoulders of the highway. Like crows, they are scavengers, and help clean-up roadside pizza: fauna flattened by speeding autos.

To identify a raven, look closely for a "goiter" of shaggy throat feathers. Mature ravens also have heavier bills and are about one-third larger than crows. Their flight is like a hawk's, with much soaring, whereas a crow usually flaps its wings. Ravens have a wedge-shaped tail—the crow's is rounded.

Ravens can be found almost anywhere, from haunted castles to park townsites. Being the most intelligent of perching birds, these black scavengers thrive on our wastefulness. Yet, just like us, they need to get away occasionally and can often be seen soaring over the highest peaks. Even ravens need wild places.

Photos Bob Hahn.

127

The largest woodpecker in the Canadian Rockies is the pileated.

Woody Woodpecker, in Person?

If you spot a large, long-billed, redheaded bird you might think it's Woody Woodpecker in the flesh (or feathers). You'd also be showing your age. Kids today have so many cartoon characters to choose from that crazy woodpeckers get lost in the shuffle.

The proper name for this crow-size bird is pileated woodpecker. It's the largest woodpecker in the Canadian Rockies, and has a correspondingly loud, raucous cry, much as you would expect from a bird that size (38 cm). The Woody-look-alike is also a jackhammer with feathers who can really make the chips fly from a dead or dying tree. I've actually seen the birds stand on the ground to work as if they got a better toe-hold there. Thus the resulting holes, which are usually very deep and characteristically oval to rectangular in shape, are frequently found at the base of trees. It's much easier to find them than the shy bird itself.

Holes chiseled by pileated woodpeckers are usually rectangular in shape. Photo Bob Hahn.

The woodpeckers are drilling for carpenter ants, but to be successful they use more than a sharp beak. They have a long, slender tongue to probe into the ant condominiums and extract the residents. The tongue may be extended up to four inches beyond the end of the bill. Sticky saliva along with barbs at the end of the tongue are used to retrieve the insects.

Long tongues are essential to pileated woodpeckers, but the problem is how to store them when not in use? In most birds, the two bones that tongue muscles are attached to end at the trachea. Woodpeckers need more room. Therefore, their tongue supports continue up over the top of the skull and down between their eyes, terminating in the right nostril. Maybe that's why Woody has such a crazy "laugh"—a tongue stored in the nose might really tickle.

Cutthroat trout are native to park waters. Photo Bob Hahn.

Finny Fauna

Game fish found in the park include four species that we refer to as trout: cutthroat, rainbow, eastern brook and bull trout (formerly Dolly Varden), plus Rocky Mountain whitefish. The whitefish are often confused with grayling, but there are no grayling in Kootenay waters.

Brook trout and bull trout are actually char, but the difference between char and the other trout isn't all that important to most people. What is essential is that anglers be able to differentiate between brookies and bulls because all bull trout must be released. A disastrous reduction in their population has occurred over most of western North America (see page xx). Destruction of habitat is probably the primary cause, but overfishing has undoubtedly had an effect also. Refer to the illustrations on park fishing regulations, which show that brook trout have black spots on their dorsal (back) fin, and black lines on their pelvic, pectoral and anal fins (all on the underside of their bodies). Bull trout don't have the black on any of those areas—thus the saying, "No black, put it back."

Park fishing policies have undergone some major changes over the years, just like a lot of other policies. At one time fish were stocked in park waters with little or no understanding about the various aquatic environments. The planted fish were non-native rainbows, brook trout and even some Yellowstone cutthroat. No thought was given to the possible effect on the native west slope cutthroat trout. Unfortunately, before stocking was halted, much damage had been done and to this day we're really not sure if any of our pure-strain native cutthroats are left in Kootenay.

No stocking has occurred in the park since the early 1970s, and undoubtedly fewer fish end up in the frying pan. The main reason for allowing any fishing in park waters is to enhance visitor enjoyment, not to provide sustenance.

Studies of aquatic environments in our parks have lagged behind most other work. A concerted effort to catch up is now underway. In the meantime many regulations have been tightened to help ensure ecological integrity is as secure underwater as it is above. Limits have been reduced as well as a promotion of catch-and-release fishing (see page 76). Other regulations and open seasons are subject to change in the future as more knowledge is acquired.

Long-toed salamanders remain well hidden during most of the daylight hours.

Long-Toed Sally

Only one kind of salamander, the long-toed type, is found in Kootenay National Park. Of all the amphibians, salamanders have always fascinated me the most, because they are mainly nocturnal and thus aren't seen as often as their relatives, the toads and frogs. However, as amphibian populations decline in the world, it's not even as easy to find a frog as it used to be.

Kootenay's only salamander species is about 80-120 mm long, with an oval head and blunt snout. The eyes are large, with bronze-tinged irises. The slender body is greenish-gray to black, with a stem-to-stern, yellow dorsal stripe and white flecks on the sides.

Long-toed salamanders spend most of the daylight hours hiding under rocks, rotting logs and other debris. They usually aren't far from some body of water—such as Kootenay Pond. That's where mating takes place so early in the spring that the pond may still be covered with ice. The male climbs on the female and rubs his special chin glands on her snout. Then he drops a packet of sperm, which she picks up. Shortly thereafter, the eggs are laid. The tiny tadpole-like larvae transform into adults at the end of the summer or the following spring. Long-toed salamanders overwinter by burrowing up to a metre deep in the mud. Some might also be found under loose material in borrow pits.

It's a good thing fish are no longer stocked in Kootenay Pond, because salamander populations are declining fast enough without introducing predators to eat them. The decline in amphibians is a worldwide phenomenon that was initially blamed on local human influences such as deforestation, draining of wetlands and pollution. However, in 1988, herpetologists (people who study reptiles and amphibians) began reporting declines in more pristine areas such as national parks. This led to the suggestion that a number of global factors might also be having adverse effects on the amphibian populations.

Topping the list of detrimental factors that may be affecting the thin-skinned creatures worldwide are increased ultraviolet radiation and pollution such as acid rain. The skin of an amphibian is so permeable they can breathe through it. Just think about all the complaints related to second-hand smoke in our society. What if you could absorb smoke through your skin, as well as through your lungs? The incidence of cancer would likely skyrocket. Polluted air, pesticides and a variety of other damaging chemicals can easily cause a lot of sick froggies.

And who hasn't heard about the hole in the ozone layer and the need to lather on sunscreen whenever we go outdoors? Pity the poor amphibians. Who doctors their sunburns? Many extreme population declines have been noted at high altitudes where atmospheric protection is minimal.

What might cause you to take the decline of amphibians more seriously is knowing how long frogs, toads and salamanders have survived on earth. They waited 150 million years before sending out the Welcome Wagon to dinosaurs—and you know the dinos have been gone a long time. We aren't sure what caused Tyrannosaurus rex and friends to disappear and we're not exactly sure what's causing the decrease in amphibians. As with most population changes, a combination of factors is probably to blame.

It should be obvious that, with few exceptions, the environmental factors mentioned above are also detrimental to human life. We are working to rectify our mistakes, but if we end up saying good-bye to the salamanders, it might mean we're doing too little, too late. And if frogs and salamanders disappear, who's next?

Kootenay's Boa

Boa constrictors in the Rocky Mountains! Impossible, you say—but it's true. Rubber boas are infrequently found in the vicinity of the Radium Hot Springs Pools. I've only seen one, and it was delivered to me by a pair of boys who said they found the reptile on the Redstreak Campground trail. Unfortunately, it was already in the state that misguided youth often leave creepy-crawly creatures—dead.

There is no need to fear rubber boas, even though they are true constrictors who squeeze the life out of their prey. However, as maximum size of the snakes is about 85 cm, only mice, unwary birds and other small creatures are in danger. If you picked up a rubber boa, it would probably just curl up and lie motionless in your hand.

Rubber boas don't even look real. They are chocolate brown with a blunt enough tail to make you wonder which end is which. Reported sightings are rare as the snakes aren't common and they are also nocturnal. I wonder how many casual visitors would actually bother to investigate a boa closely instead of just mentally noting that some child had lost their toy snake?

Rubber boas look more like chocolate-coloured toys than real snakes. Courtesy Kootenay National Park. Photo Larry Halverson.

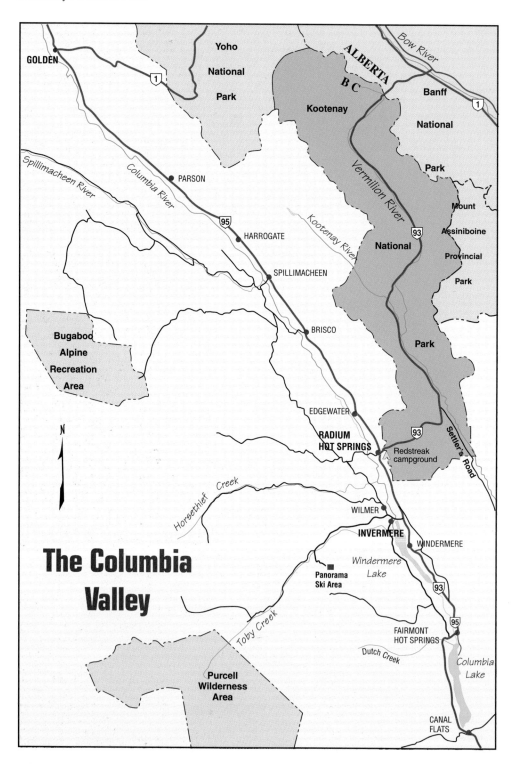

The Columbia Valley

The Columbia Valley

Columbia Lake is the source of the mighty Columbia River. Photo Bob Hahn.

Sunk in the Trench—Canal Flats to Golden

Near the southern terminus of the Columbia Valley lies the hamlet of **Canal Flats**, sandwiched between the Kootenay River and Columbia Lake. From the highway, the residential area seems dwarfed by a large sawmill. Located beyond town, on the east shore of Columbia Lake, is Canal Flats Provincial Park (day use).

As you head north on Highway 93/95, remnants of the canal itself (see page 142) and an information sign can be seen just before the highway starts up a long grade. Sideroads lead west to the Findlay Creek drainage (watch for the Blue Lake Forestry Centre sign at the top of the grade), an expansive area of wilderness, wildlife and good fishing.

The highway climbs to a bench above Columbia Lake, which it parallels for most of the way to Dutch Creek, the source of much of the water in the fledgling Columbia River. Rising just north of the rushing creek, like a many-turreted cas-

The Columbia Wetlands stretches south from the Springs Golf Course in Radium Hot Springs. Photo Bob Hahn.

tle, are the Dutch Creek hoodoos. The hoodoos have been carved from silty, gravelly sediments by water. According to Ktunaxa legend, the hoodoos are the ribs of a giant fish that never quite made it up the water-filled trench.

Located around the corner from the hoodoos, just beyond a small pocket of civilization where you can gas up, buy pizza and ice cream cones or find a campsite, is the junction of a hard-topped secondary road. This is the Westside Road, an alternate route to Invermere.

The main highway soon crosses the Columbia River and reaches **Fairmont Hot Springs**. On your left is a golf course, one of two 18-holers in this resort area. If your main obsession in life is to chase little white balls, there is no shortage of courses in the valley. A long-ball hitter could start here and play almost all the way north to Radium Hot Springs.

serves as an artists' studio. A variety of artists including glass-blowers, wood carvers and printmakers find their inspiration in this quiet lakeside village.

Left: Fairmont boasts of the largest hot pool in Canada. Photo Bob Hahn.

Right: St. Peter's Anglican Church in Windermere is commonly referred to as the Stolen Church because of its colourful history. Photo Bob Hahn.

Fairmont also boasts the largest hot pool (there are actually three pools) in Canada. Unfortunately, visitors who come to bathe in the main attraction, the springs, never actually see them—but the same is true in Kootenay National Park and other areas with hot springs. Natural pools just can't accommodate the thousands of people who enjoy soaking in the mineral-rich water. And those thousands of bodies are also going to affect the purity of the water, so appropriate sanitary measures must be taken.

As you continue north, glimpses of Windermere Lake appear through the trees to the west. This lake is the watery playground that helps attract enough summer visitors to cause the valley's year-round population to multiply five-fold in the warmer months. Smallest of two communities on the lake is **Windermere**, the oldest white settlement on the upper Columbia. Windermere is mostly a residential area, but in 1887 it boasted a hotel—with two rooms for rent—a store and the government building. Today, the renovated store

The most famous building in Windermere is St. Peter's Anglican Church, the first Protestant church built in the Kootenays. It is also commonly called the Stolen Church. The little church originally stood at Donald, about 125 km north of Windermere, when the Canadian Pacific Railway was under construction. After the railway was completed, Donald became a ghost town. Rufus and Celina Kimpton moved to Windermere, but Celina dearly missed her church. Rufus hated to see his wife so unhappy. Thus, he enlisted the aid of a few friends, dismantled the church and shipped it south. The first part of the journey was by rail to Golden. At that point the Golden Anglicans appropriated the bell, but the building continued on to Windermere by barge. The Kimptons could say little about the loss of the bell as the transfer of the church had never been sanctioned by anyone of authority. Windermere churchgoers were very patient. They waited until the Golden church belfry needed repairs and the bell had been removed. Then, under the

Right: A tube-like structure now prevents ospreys from nesting on this pole. Photo Bob Hahn.

Far right: Nature apologizes for a thunderstorm with this brilliant rainbow seen from James Chabot Provincial Park. Photo Bob Hahn.

cover of darkness, they spirited the bell away—60 years after the original move. The church is now open to visitors. Check the sign outside for hours.

Watch for a power pole topped by a platform on the east side of the highway opposite the north access to Windermere. The huge pile of sticks on top is an osprey nest that continues to grow from yearly additions. For most of the summer at least one of the white-headed fish-eaters is present. B.C. Hydro erected a number of osprey highrises in hopes of preventing the birds from nesting on power poles. The birds' preference for those unnatural vantage points was causing regular summer power outages. Bird-caused electrical problems are now rare.

The turnoff for **Invermere**, shopping hub of the valley, is reached a few kilometres beyond Windermere. It is marked by a set of stop lights and a sign extolling the attractions of this popular, expanding area. One of the newest attractions is a golf course and resort on your right next to the airport. As

you wind down the hill, with the outlet from the lake on your left, look for an orange and white striped power pole on the opposite side of the bridge. You'll notice a strange tube-like structure on top. This addition became necessary when ospreys continued to nest on their traditional site—the colourful pole—ignoring the nearby platform that had been constructed for them. Hydro crews had to wait until the birds abandoned their nest for the season and then transferred the sticks to the platform.

The collection of buildings beyond the bridge is known as **Athalmer**. During the early part of the century this was a prosperous little settlement with two banks, two hotels, a customs office, a newspaper and other businesses. Athalmer was a distribution centre for goods coming up the Columbia by steamboat and barge. You can still see pilings from the old wharves north of the bridge.

Long before the bridge was built the area was called the Salmon Beds after the fish that crowded the riffles every fall. Aboriginal peoples came as regularly as the fish to build their *keekwillies*. The keekwillies were pits in the ground covered by poles, skins and dirt. One type was used for smoking and storing salmon and a second provided shelter for the winter. The early white settlers found the salmon so numerous that one said, "All ya needed to cross the river was a pair a pitchforks. Ya just looked fer three salmon in a row, stuck a pitchfork inta the two outside fish an' hopped on the one in the middle. They'd take ya across."

At the Athalmer crossroads is a road leading left to James Chabot Provincial Park. On hot summer days the sandy beach is crammed with scantily dressed people who don't seem to be too concerned about the hole in the ozone layer. Warmer water temperatures make swimming in Windermere Lake much more pleasurable than the glacier-fed ponds found in the surrounding mountains.

A second public access to the lake is Kinsmen Beach, south of the Invermere business area. Nearby are tennis courts, a ball diamond and the Pynelogs Cultural Centre. The centre is busiest in the summer months offering classes such as pottery-making and painting. It also serves as a gallery and sales outlet for local artists. Touring musicians are often featured in evening performances. Behind Pynelogs is tiny Dorothy Lake, noted for its fountain, turtles and osprey nesting platform.

West of Invermere is a vast area of mountains, lakes, forests and a confusing array of logging roads. Anyone wishing to explore beyond the paved roads should stop at the local B.C. Forest Service office and ask for a copy of the district's recreation map. Or purchase a copy of *Hikes Around Invermere* by Aaron

Top: Fall colours near Brisco. Photo Bob Hahn.

Left: A lazy cruise down the Columbia River below Windermere Lake is a good way to relax. Photo Bob Hahn.

Cameron and Matt Gunn at the Friends of Kootenay shop.

Up the hill from Athalmer is the turnoff for the main route to the backcountry and Panorama Resort. Eighteen kilometres of winding, pitted, but hard-topped road lead to this year-round attraction. It's most known for skiing—take your choice of downhill, cross-country or heli. Beyond this "last outpost of civilization" the now-gravel road leads to many kilometres of scenic country, home to moose and other wild creatures, with some exciting hiking trails to explore.

Just past the Toby Creek bridge a branch of the Panorama road

Harvest time in the Columbia Valley north of Radium Hot Springs. Photo Bob Hahn.

leads to the tiny residential community of **Wilmer** whose origin dates back to 1896. At that time it consisted of little more than a packhorse corral used by prospectors seeking their fortunes in nearby creeks. But by 1889 the survey for a townsite was completed, and the first store was built. Soon the village contained about 100 people, primarily miners, prospectors and cowboys. Drinking and gambling were the main pastimes, with the latter so popular the only hotel often couldn't handle all the poker players. The overflow was forced to play on the streets.

It shouldn't be necessary to dodge any poker players as you drive through Wilmer now. To the west of town are a number of lakes including Lake Enid, noted for its large, infrequently-caught rainbow trout. The main road continues north after Wilmer as a continuation of the Westside Road. Wilmer Marsh, the first unit in the Columbia National Wildlife Area (see page 142), can be seen to the right.

The now-unpaved and dusty Westside Road can be followed north all the way to Spillimacheen, with connecting roads to Radium Hot Springs and Brisco. If you turn west on any of the numerous logging roads, be prepared for adventure (see page 137).

Back to Highway 93/95, beyond the Invermere turnoff, the next stop is **Radium Hot Springs** (see page 27), unless you succumb to the attractions of par-three golf, go-carts or other tourist-oriented businesses. Several commercial campgrounds and the more-secluded Dry Gulch Provincial Park are located en route. Shortly before you start downhill into Radium, a sign beckons you to the Springs at Radium Golf Resort, a favourite of those chasers of the dimpled white ball. A second fine course, the Springs, is located on the west edge of the village. Both courses unin-

Fog lifts from the Springs Golf Course on an autumn morning. Photo Bob Hahn.

This abandoned house near Edgewater is a favourite subject for photographers. Photo Bob Hahn.

tentionally provide forage for bighorn sheep in the winter.

If you don't follow Highway 93 east into Kootenay Park, the next community north of Radium is **Edgewater**, so named because of its proximity to the Columbia River. Numerous farms and ranches line the highway, and the Columbia wetlands stretch westward from their boundaries to the base of the Purcells.

Eighteen kilometres farther north lies **Brisco**, most notable as a jumping-off point for the Bugaboos (see page 144). This area is known to mountaineers the world over, but it's well worth driving the rough gravel road west (watch for the Bugaboo Glacier Provincial Park sign) even if you don't want any exercise. There aren't many places where you can sit in your vehicle and enjoy a spectacle as grand as Bugaboo Glacier with granite spires rising above the ice.

Follow the same road from Brisco over the Columbia River to reach a multitude of forest service campsites on sparkling wilderness lakes. Before crossing the river, the road passes ponds located in an-

other unit of the Columbia National Wildlife Area. Beyond the river is more marshy habitat, where Canada geese, ducks, grebes, yellow-headed blackbirds and other feathered residents raise their young. In spring and fall, watch for large flocks of migrating tundra swans resting in such places.

One interesting stop just north of Brisco on Highway 95 is the oldest Protestant church in the East Kootenays: St. Mark's Anglican Church. St. Mark's was built in 1896 as a nondenominational place of worship and didn't officially become an Anglican church for 50 years. It's especially picturesque in the autumn, hiding among the yellow-leaved aspens. Watch closely to the east of the highway as the church is one of the smallest anywhere.

Next up the road is **Spillimacheen**, and still another section of the Columbia National Wildlife Area. Cross the bridge to link up with the north end of the Westside Road.

The northernmost unit of the Columbia National Wildlife Area lies west of **Harrogate**, a "don't blink your eyes or you'll miss it" settlement. The ponds here offer terrific birding. Then comes **Parson**, which is another good place to head west for some excellent camping and fishing areas. Watch for nesting platforms in the marshes all through this area.

The wetlands don't stop at **Golden**, but I'm going to. Highway 95 connects with the Trans-Canada Highway just beyond this railroad centre. Turn left for Rogers Pass, Glacier and Revelstoke national parks, and points west. To the east lies Yoho and Banff national parks, and the loop back through Kootenay.

The Last Wild Stretch of the Columbia

Wilmer Marsh is the first unit in the Columbia National Wildlife Area. Photo Bob Hahn.

Many visitors from the northwestern states are surprised to find themselves driving along the Columbia River on their way to Kootenay National Park. And they are even more surprised to see it flowing north. The Columbia actually begins its journey to salt water by flowing "the wrong way" for the first 175 km—trapped in the Rocky Mountain Trench.

Pinpointing the actual source of the Columbia is not easy. Most of the water could probably be traced to Dutch Creek, which is crossed by Highway 93, just south of Fairmont Hot Springs. However, there is no question the stream flowing out of Columbia Lake is the same one that drains into the Pacific Ocean at Astoria, Oregon, 2000 km downstream—except for its character. It's born a fast-running, clear stream

that quickly disappears into busy Windermere Lake, site of summer homes and associated aquatic activities. When the river flees the hustle and bustle of the lake, it still runs clear, but that doesn't last long. Once silt-laden Toby Creek roars in from the Purcell Mountains, the Columbia changes from sparkling blue to drab brown.

Wrong direction isn't the only thing unusual about this end of the Columbia. A short walk 1.5 km south from Columbia Lake near the village of Canal Flats ends on the banks of the Kootenay River, one of the Columbia's main tributaries. However, the two rivers don't actually meet until the Kootenay passes through Koocanusa Reservoir, formed by Montana's Libby Dam, and then flows north, back into British Columbia near the town of Castlegar. Castlegar is 320 km via highway and two mountain ranges away from Canal Flats.

The unusual proximity of the two rivers at McGillivray's Portage, as the area was first named, prompted a wealthy Englishman, W. A. Baillie-Grohman, to execute a scheme to join the waterways. His decision was based on the realization that 19,000 ha of alluvial flats in what is now the Creston area would become valuable agricultural land if they weren't flooded by the Kootenay River every spring. Diverting water from the river to nearby Columbia Lake would end the flooding. However, when residents of the upper Columbia Valley learned that Baillie-Grohman's project had been approved by the British Columbia government, they objected, claiming the diversion would simply transfer the high-water problems to them. Then the Canadian Pacific Railway complained that the new CPR tracks along the Columbia near Golden would be flooded. Eventually, the B.C. government specified the canal-work could proceed only if a lock was also constructed.

After much consideration Baillie-Grohman decided to go ahead with the amended plan. Backed by a London syndicate, he issued picks and shovels to Chinese labourers, and they began hacking out a 2000 m-long canal. By constructing a deep waterway, 14 m wide, and installing the lock, it became possible for small steamboats to move between the two rivers. However, after the canal was completed in 1889, only two steamboats ever traversed it. It took two weeks for the 40 m-long North Star to squeeze through in 1902. The clever captain had to burn the narrow wooden locks and then replace them with sandbags. When the water level reached sufficient depth behind the barrier it was blown up and the North Star rode the resulting surge of water triumphantly down to Columbia Lake. A discouraged Baillie-Grohman had abandoned his canal and returned to England almost 10 years earlier, so no one objected to the destruction.

Remnants of the canal are still visible, but to the casual observer they simply appear to be more of the wetlands that characterize the upper Columbia. These 26,000 ha of marsh, boggy meadows, swamps, ponds and islands crowned by willows and cottonwoods provide ideal habitat for at least 200 different species of vertebrates. As you might expect, this huge wetland is of worldwide importance, and has offically been recognized as such.

The Canadian Wildlife Service has set aside four wildlife refuges between Invermere and the little town of Harrogate as the Columbia

A researcher of the Canadian Wildlife Service places a band on one of 15,000 ducks that use the Columbia Wetlands. Photo Bob Hahn.

National Wildlife Area. As you might expect, the primary objective is to protect migrating birds. As many as 15,000 ducks have been recorded along the upper river during a single fall migration. The CWS does the autumn count, and also bands birds in July when they are moulting and thus easily captured. Almost anywhere on the river you can hear honking calls coming from one or more of the 1200 pairs of Canada geese that nest there. Nesting boxes on platforms, built to encourage their breeding, are often visible from the highway north of Harrogate.

When drifting down the Columbia on a warm Sunday, I know I'll see nesting ospreys (the area has one of the highest osprey populations in the world), perhaps investigate a patch of cotton grass on the shore, and definitely lie back in the canoe to savour the unique fragrance of this wild river. On one trip, we swung around the corner of a slow-moving back channel and were startled out of our lethargy by splashes from a departing mother moose and her offspring. Mallards rose from the reeds, females quacking at the double interruption.

Interruptions on a float are an exception. You rarely even have to use paddles—unless the wind blows from the north. With an average drop of only 10 cm to the mile, the upper Columbia is ideal for novice canoeists. While the most strenuous exertions of the majority of floaters may be the application of sunscreen, the more intrepid types are hauling canoes over beaver dams in a maze of back channels. They may even have to portage cross-country when a promising waterway dead-ends. But a brief dip in the cold water quickly washes away the sweat and fosters an appreciation of the hot sun, which shines most of the time.

Precipitation is light, because the Columbia Valley lies in the rain shadow of the Purcell and Selkirk mountains to the west. This lack of snow makes the bottomlands important winter range for elk and deer. Obviously, protection of the wetlands is also vital to many other species of wildlife.

Bird studies have been continuing for many years, but they aren't the only research going on in the valley. In fact, an increase in funding as compensation for loss of habitat owing to flooding behind dams on the Columbia has prompted a variety of projects. A sampling of recent research includes studies about bats, bighorn sheep, cottonwood trees, wolverines, amphibians and even the feasibility of introducing bass into riverside ponds.

While canoeing on the Columbia, expect startling encounters with beavers. It's quite a thrill to be gliding downstream at twilight, in a semi-trance from the combination of alpenglow on the mountains and the gentle murmuring of the silt-laden water, when one of the large rodents announces its presence with a shattering slap of his frying pan tail—it's a heart-stopping gift from this aqueous giant called Columbia.

Elsewhere, the mighty Columbia may be tamed by dams, but here it still runs wild and free—a treasure to be revered by the whole world.

Bugaboo Glacier is most spectacular when viewed from the trail to the Conrad Kain Alpine Hut. Photo Bob Hahn.

Ancestors of the Rockies

British Columbia is full of mountain ranges, of which the Rockies is only one. And the Rockies are "the new kids on the block," because most of the other ranges were growing whiskers before the Rockies came on the scene.

One such range is the Purcell Mountains, which rise dramatically to the west of the Columbia Valley. Eroded sediment from the Purcells can be seen in the foothills of the Rockies, 100 km to the east (see page 19).

While the Rocky Mountain national parks have to be the number-one international attraction in the region, the Purcells also have fans worldwide. Mention Bugaboos to any knowledgable mountaineer and his/her eyes will light up. Since the 1920s, this rugged region of glaciers and granite spires has attracted climbers from all over the globe. Other visitors are quite willing to brave the 45 km of rough gravel road west from the hamlet of Brisco just to view spectacular Bugaboo Glacier as it tumbles down from the lofty peaks.

Sometimes the tranquillity is shattered by a helicopter bearing guests from Bugaboo Lodge, out for a day of heli-hiking or skiing, depending on the season. This often prompts some grumbling from the hikers who come to Bugaboo Glacier Provincial Park to enjoy the spectacular wilderness vistas of flowers, ice and blue sky. However, for some of the less-able passengers on the 'copters, flying is the only way they may ever experience the alpine.

The most popular hiking trail climbs 700 m in 5 km along the lateral moraine of the glacier to Conrad Kain Alpine Hut. Kain was the area's most famous guide, who led the first ascent of Bugaboo Spire in 1916. He and two companions were also the first mountaineers to climb Mount Robson, the highest peak in the Canadian Rockies. Another favourite trail is the even steeper route to Cobalt Lake (5 km, elevation gain 884 m).

The Bugs are not the only international attraction in the Purcells. Lake of the Hanging Glacier is a popular destination, especially for photographers. It is reached via Horsethief Creek road, west of Radium Hot Springs. The hike to the lake is 3 km longer, but not as demanding as those in the Bugaboos. However, the scenic reward—especially the icebergs in the lake—is equally impressive.

There are many other lovely lakes scattered among the peaks, and some can be reached by car. Primitive Forest Service campsites are often located on the shores, thus allowing visitors to enjoy a weekend of fishing for rainbow and cutthroat trout, or just lazing amidst quiet outdoor splendour. You'll likely find even more solitude, and some good fishing, by hiking up some of the streams, like Frances or Findlay creeks. Choose your destinations carefully along the latter, because there are some steep-walled canyons that are best viewed far above the creek.

Shangri-la, Earl Grey Pass, Paradise Mine, Welsh Lakes, Jumbo Pass, the Septet Range, Chalice Creek—they are all there, waiting to be explored. Arm yourself with a Forest Service map and brochures, then set out to explore the beauty of the Purcells. Better plan on taking a few years, though. There's a lot to see.

Climbers have long been attracted to the granite spires of the Bugaboos. Photo Bob Hahn.

Below: Lake of the Hanging Glacier is one of the most popular hiking destinations in the Purcells. Photo Bob Hahn.

The Birdman of Kootenay—Larry Halverson

Park naturalist Larry Halverson has been chasing birds in the Columbia Valley and vicinity since 1972, when he began work in Kootenay National Park. Halverson's fanaticism with the feathered songsters isn't a selfish pursuit. He delights in sharing his extensive knowledge with those of us less schooled in avian ways. Thousands of students in British Columbia have benefitted from Halverson's insights, as have bird watchers from across the globe.

It doesn't come easy. As the saying goes: "The early bird gets the worm"—and the early bird watcher spots the most birds. It's not unusual for Larry to rise before dawn and spend several hours afield before attending to his national-park duties. His wife, five children and faithful dog Hunter all realize they can't separate the man from his feathered friends. Many now come to participate in the annual Wings Over the Rockies Bird Festival, which he helped found.

~

Here are some of Larry's views on the local birdwatching scene:

"British Columbia has about 450 species of birds. With a little patience and lots of luck you might eventually see 271 of them in the

The Halverson homestead on the Columbia River near Brisco. Photo Bob Hahn.

Columbia Valley. In the spring it's not unusual to record 100 species in a single day.

"Some bird watchers are really keen on learning all about the different species, and others are what we call tickers. They just want to tick birds off their lists—the faster, the better. Show them a grizzly bear and they'll just say, 'Get that fur outta the way!'

"Among some of the more unusual birds in the area are Lewis' woodpeckers, often found in the Dutch Creek burn, and the veery, a type of thrush with a unique song—sounds like its name coming through a tube. Another unusual visitor is the long-billed curlew, occasionally seen in cultivated fields.

"This is also a good place to get a grand slam in chickadees! Of course, the black-capped and mountain chickadees are pretty common. Then we have the boreal at higher elevations. Rarest is the chestnut-backed. You know you've had a good day when you've picked up the grand slam.

"The Wilmer Marsh is one of the best areas to find a variety of birds. Not only does it have great waterfowl habitat, but the open dry grassland found there is rare in the province. It's a good place to find vesper sparrows, western meadowlarks and mountain bluebirds. The bluebirds often show up as early as the first week of March.

"Peak time for waterfowl is about the third week of April. But tundra swans—they used to be called whistling swans—are staging in the area by early March.

"The most prominent raptors are bald eagles and ospreys. There is an eagle migration in the spring, and eagles can be seen packing sticks for nests in February. We have the second highest concentration of ospreys in B.C.—the Creston area is number one.

"A great time to look for birds is just prior to daybreak, because they're very active then. One of the best places to visit at that time is along the Columbia River or its backwaters. The mill pond at Radium is good. It's easy to get to and has a wonderful assortment of birds—red-necked grebes, ring-necked ducks and even wood ducks.

"Another good area is near Brisco (see page 139). One small slough has black terns, every variety of teal, ruddy ducks and yellow-headed blackbirds. Look for the blackbirds when you hear a sound like someone being strangled.

"One key element for bird life in the valley bottom is the abundance of huge poplars and cottonwoods, especially old snags. After the pileated woodpeckers excavate big holes in them, the snags become homes for cavity nesters such as goldeneyes, buffleheads and mergansers.

~

"My most embarrassing bird–watching experience came one evening when I was out with a lady biologist from the Canadian Wildlife Service doing an owl survey. We'd parked on a side road near Wilmer, and had the windows down and lights off. A pygmy owl was hooting just above us.

"A car came up from behind with its bright lights on. Wanting to keep my eyes acclimated to the dark, I held my arm in front of my face and kind of ducked down. The car went on by, but quickly spun around, came up to my side and out popped an RCMP constable.

"He came over and asked, 'Having any trouble?'

"Before I could say anything, my companion leaned over and said,

'Oh no, officer. We're just listening to owls—little pygmy owls.'

"There was a twinkle in the officer's eye as he turned away, 'Well, O.K. Have a nice evening.'

~

"One of my fondest memories as a park naturalist concerns a family who came to the park years ago when their son was only eight. They always went on guided walks and they came to the different evening programs. We enjoyed the annual visits, and our friendship grew to the point that after the son graduated from university, he and I went on a backpacking trip together.

"It's satisfying to know that you've had some influence on people's attitudes about the park and the environment. If folks have good experiences in the wild, those memories might come to mind when landscapes are threatened— making those same people defenders of the places they cherish. It makes it all worthwhile."

There is no more dedicated bird-lover than Larry Halverson.

Addresses and Phone Numbers

Administration:

Kootenay National Park
Box 220
Radium Hot Springs, B.C. VOA 1M0
Phone: (250) 347-9615
FAX: (250) 347-9980
email: Park_reception@pch.gc.ca
Internet site: www.worldweb.com/ParksCanada-Kootenay

Kootenay warden office (non emergency): (250) 347-9361

Kootenay **emergency** calls—Banff dispatch: (403) 762-4506

Radium Hot Springs Pools: (250) 347-9485

Radium Information Centre: (250) 347-9505 (June-Oct.)

Lake Louise Information Centre: (403) 522-3833

For information on the local area:

Village of Radium Hot Springs
P.O. Box 340
Radium Hot Springs, B.C. VOA 1M0
Phone: (250) 347-6455
FAX: (250) 347-9068
email: village@RadiumHotSprings.com

Radium Hot Springs Visitor Information Centre (April-Nov.)
Box 225
Radium Hot Springs, B.C. VOA 1M0
Phone: (250) 347-9331
toll free: 1-800-347-9704
FAX: (250) 347-9127
email: info@radiumhotsprings.com
Internet: www.radiumhotsprings.com

For other information on British Columbia contact:

Tourism British Columbia
300-1803 Douglas St.
Victoria, B.C. V8W 9W5
Phone toll free: 1-800-435-5622
Internet site: www.travel.bc.ca/

Recommended Reading

Burt, W. H. and R. P. Grossenheider. *Mammals*. Boston: Houghton Mifflin, 3rd edition, 1980.

Cameron, Aaron and Matt Gunn. *Hikes around Invermere and the Columbia River Valley*. Calgary: Rocky Mountain Books, 1998.

Daffern, Tony. *Avalanche Safety for Skiers, Climbers & Snowboarders*. Calgary: Rocky Mountain Books, 1999.

Dougherty, Sean. *Selected Alpine Climbs in the Canadian Rockies*. Calgary: Rocky Mountain Books, 1996.

Fraser, Esther. *The Canadian Rockies: Early Travels and Explorations*. Edmonton: M. G. Hurtig Ltd., 1969.

Gadd, Ben. *Handbook of the Canadian Rockies*. Jasper: Corax Press, 2nd edition, 1995.

Herrero, S. *Bear Attacks: Their Causes and Avoidance*. Piscataway, New Jersey: New Century, 1985.

Kane, Alan. *Scrambles in the Canadian Rockies*. Calgary: Rocky Mountain Books, 1999.

Lemaster, Denise. *Columbia Valley Guide*. Banff: Luminous Compositions, 1997.

MacKinnon, A., J. Pojar and R. Coupe. *Plants of Northern British Columbia*. Edmonton: Lone Pine Publishing, 1993.

Marty, Sid. *A Grand and Fabulous Notion*. Toronto: NC Press, 1984.

Patton, Brian and Bart Robinson. *Canadian Rockies Trail Guide*. Banff: Summerthought, 1994.

Peterson, R. T. *A Field Guide to the Western Birds*. Boston: Houghton Mifflin, 3rd edition, 1989.

Pole, Graeme. *Walks and Easy Hikes in the Canadian Rockies*. Banff: Altitude Publishing, 1992.

Pole, Graeme. *Classic Hikes in the Canadian Rockies*. Banff/Canmore: Altitude Publishing, 1994.

Porsild, A. E. and D. T. Lid. *Rocky Mountain Wildflowers*. Ottawa: National Museum of Natural Sciences, 1979.

Scott, Chic. *Ski Trails in the Canadian Rockies*. Calgary: Rocky Mountain Books, 1998.

Scotter, G. W. and H. Flygare. *Wildflowers of the Canadian Rockies*. Toronto: McLelland and Stewart, 1992.

Index

Emergency Phone Numbers

RCMP (Radium Hot Springs)	(250) 347-9393
Invermere	(250) 342-9292
Ambulance (Invermere)	(250) 342-2055
Hospital (Invermere)	(250) 342-9201
Hospital (Banff)	(403) 762-2222
Towing (Radium Esso)	(250) 347-9726
Fire	(250) 347-9333
Forest Fire	1-800-663-5555

Emergency calls to warden service—Banff dispatch: (403) 762-4506

Location of Phones Within the Park

Kootenay Crossing—radiophone, for emergencies only
Vermilion Crossing—Kootenay Park Lodge
Banff National Park—Storm Mountain Lodge

Easy Metric/Imperial Conversions (approximate)

Centimetres (cm) to inches	Divide cm by 2.5
Metres (m) to feet	Multiply m x 3.3
Kilometres (km) to miles	Multiply km x 0.6
Hectares (ha) to acres	Multiply ha by 2.5
Kilograms (kg) to pounds	Multiply kg by 2.2
Litres (l) to US gallons	Divide l by 4

Temperature
Fahrenheit = 9/5 Celsius + 32, so an easy approximate conversion is
2 x C + 30 = F
Thus:
0°C = ~30°F (actually 32°F)
5°C = ~40°F (actually 41°F)
10°C = 50°F
15°C = ~60°F (actually 59°F)
20°C = ~70°F (actually 68°F)
25°C = ~80°F (actually 77°F)
30°C = ~90°F (actually 86°F)